SOUTHERN WAY

WARTIME SOUTHERN PART 3

Spe

CW00421640

Introduction, Acknowledgments and Bibliography	3
Watching Trains on the Southern: September 1942 - July 1945	5
'Feeding the 5000'. Dover and Headcorn: June 1940	33
1940 Difficult Days	34
1941 Back to the Blitz	46
Examples of SR Coaching Stock used for WD Purposes	49
1941 Back to the Blitz - continued	50
1944 The Flying Bombs	57
1945 St Mary Cray	74
The Scene Behind the Scene	77
The Air Raid and Occurrence Logs	84
Individual Occurrence Reports	87
The Evacuation that Never Was	94
The Lighter Side	96
Feedback	99

© Kevin Robertson (Noodle Books) and the various contributors 2011

ISBN 978-1-906419-55-4

First published in 2011 by Kevin Robertson

under the **NOODLE BOOKS** imprint

PO Box 279

Corhampton

SOUTHAMPTON

SO32 3Z

www.noodlebooks.co.uk

editorial@thesouthernway.co.uk

Printed in England by

Ian Allan Printing Ltd

Hersham, Surrey

HOLIDAY WARNING

WAR TRAINS

come before

HOLIDAY TRAINS

During the August holiday limited services only will be run.

STAY AT HOME

You may be stranded if you travel.

BRITISH RAILWAYS

GWR LMS LNER SR

Above - Some of the 300,000 saved from Dunkirk. Defeated (fortunately temporarily, although at the time referred to as a 'strategic withdrawal') soldiers with little more than the uniform they stand up in being resupplied with food at Headcorn on their way to various billets around the country. 2 June 1940. See also pages 34/35.

Left - One of a series of posters produced for the railway companies in WW2: this one to emphasize the fact certain trains would have priority over passenger workings. (Other in the series appear on page 33.)

Editorial Introduction

In this the final part of the 'Southern at War' series we are delighted to present a different perspective to the earlier volumes. Indeed if I had been asked me in the summer of 2007 if there would even be a first book, the answer would have been an emphatic 'No'. It was only through the kindness of the then photographic archivist of the Railway, Canal & Historic Society, Stephen Duffel, that the secrets of an incredible archive were made available. Subsequently I was fortunate enough to make contact with numerous others having like interest, most notably Ben Brooksbank, and it is to these two gentlemen especially that I record my grateful thanks. Many others have also contributed material without which this volume could never have appeared. They are annotated accordingly.

Compared with the previous books in the series which have been primarily photographic, this last book deliberately encompasses examples of the ways of workings of the period, as well as observations from that time, both of which interspersed with contemporary photographs. There are also examples of the bravery portrayed by ordinary men and women as well as witness statements to the describe the actions of the enemy and those affected. I say this is the last book in the series, for whilst at the conclusion of the last two there was a private thought that there might well be another should there be the demand, I can truthfully say that the 'Southern Way' special for 2012 will be on a totally different topic.

Despite also my comments about this book taking more of a look behind the scene, I will admit the three volumes in the series have never set out to be a full history of the Southern Railway between 1939 and 1945. Instead I leave that task to Ben Brooksbank, who has kindly made available his incredible archive of wartime notes on enemy action and damage which is included in a searchable PDF file contained on the CDROM at the rear of this book. Whilst there may be ongoing debate over the merits - or otherwise - of this type of electronic presentation, I think it fair to say that unless presented in this form Ben's work would otherwise have been difficult to bring to the market in commercial form. Ben's papers, some 230 pages, also refer not just to the SR during WW2, but also the GWR, LMS, LNER and LPTB. The deliberate choice was made to retain all the non SR items, as in this way the disruption to the Southern Railway can be seen in context.

The written file on the CDROM alone amounted to ten years research at the then Public Record Office (nowadays the National Archive), completed also at a time when pencil and paper was all that was permitted - research is a lot more relaxed nowadays! Then there was a further two years compilation and assimilation. It is a piece of research that will be of value to students of history for decades to come and is unlikely to be surpasses.

So far as this series of books is concerned, I am conscious that whilst we may now know far more on the difficulties of running a railway between 1939 - 1945, we are still lacking photographic information on the special trains run, both commercial and military. Consequently I am aware we have only just scratched the surface on that topic.

For all the difficulties created by the enemy, the annoyance and disruption, they singularly failed to achieve their main objective which was to permanently cut the supply lines: both military and domestic. Instead it was the staff of the Southern (and of course the other companies) who rose to the occasion, taking hours to achieve what now takes days, and to rebuild in days what we now take weeks to mend.

Perhaps the reader might keep this in mind when revisiting some of the examples of the bravery and well deserved awards subsequently made, ordinary men and women thrown into a situation most could hardly have imagined, and yet, a situation destined to bring out the very best in many. Had that bomb - or incident - occurred a few miles away on a different route, have no doubt a railwayman with a different name would have acted in similar fashion.

Kevin Robertson

ACKOWLEDGEMENTS and BIBLIOGRAPHY

Apart from those individuals and organisations referred to above and in the captions and credits, special mention must also be made to John Atkinson, Dick Coombes, Les Darbyshire, Fred Emery, Bruce Murray and Alastair Wilson, for their support and encouragement.

Three specific published works have been referred to in the compilation of this work, other more general railway titles perhaps to confirm or seek additional data.

The principal sources are:

London Main Line War Damage - B W L Brooksbank. Capital Transport.

Return from Dunkirk - Railways to the Rescue: Operation Dynamo 1940 - Peter Tatlow. The Oakwood Press, 2010.

War on the Line - Bernard Darwin. The Southern Railway.

Front cover - *Fearful of what might be on the horizon: invasion. An example of the attempt to slow the advance the enemy, Esher 1940.*

Rear cover - *Wartime travel! Four year old Christopher John Webb en-route from Fareham to Exeter. The rough black-out painting around the windows will be noted.*
C J Webb

Friday 27 December 1940 was not a good day. Two days after Christmas it might have been and official records refer to no incidents having affected the railway since the 23 December, there were not even any alerts on the 25 and 26 December. But that would all change over the 27/28 December when London suffered a 'moderate' attack of relatively short duration. On this occasion, a 'moderate' raid was deemed as 141 killed, five serious fires, and two hospitals hit. On the SR there was disruption - caused by damage - between Southwark Park Road and North Kent East Junction: at Lewisham sub-station: between Ladywell and Lewisham: between Beckenham Junction and Shortlands: at Crofton Park: at New Cross: at Penge East: at Honor Oak Park: at Bricklayers Arms Goods: at Rotherhithe Road carriage sidings: at New Cross Gate: and between North Dulwich and Tulse Hill. On this last section a heavy bomb fell a short distance inside the north portal of Knights Hill Tunnel. Forty feet of the tunnel arch was destroyed almost to rail level and a crater 50 feet deep formed in what was bad clay. This occurred at 7.50 pm, unfortunately the time the 6.30 pm circular London Bridge - London Bridge EMU service entered the tunnel and struck the debris. The motorman was trapped, it later transpired he had died instantly. The Guard was slightly injured but no passengers were hurt. Seven coaches of the train were pulled back by a locomotive although the leading coach, seen above, was left embedded. Drag line excavators were brought in to work from the top and despite being hampered by bad weather and a subsequent slip, a new concrete arch was provided, topped with three feet of filling which included some of the debris. Although it was initially hoped the work might be completed in four weeks, the damaged coach was not removed until 21 January 1941, both lines were reopened on 10 March 1941.

Ben Brooksbank collection

WATCHING TRAINS ON THE SOUTHERN 1938 - 1967

Part 1B: September 1942 - July 1945

Ben W. L. Brooksbank

The next day, **9 September**, I had another morning session (3½ hours) at **Clapham Junction**. The engine workings seen were of course much as on the previous day, comprising the following:- Waterloo line, EP/OP:- 'Merchant Navy' 21C8 'Orient Line'; N15 770 'Sir Prianius', 783 'Sir Gillemere'; T14 443, V 924 'Haileybury', 928 'Stowe'. Empty stock, carriage pilots and the like:- 0-8-0T 949 'Hecate', O2 179, 212; M7 33, 123/32, 241, 319, 667; H 1548/54. To/from WLER:- LMS 4-6-0 5240, 2-8-0 8202, 0-6-0 3261, 4021, 4345/9, 0-4-4T 1374; LNE N1 4551/5/87; GW 57XX 8751. LB&SC line (including to/from WLER):- N15 801 'Sir Meliot de Logres'; Q1 C27; C2X 2451; J1 2325; W 1915/6/9/24; I3 2024/30/81/90; E6X 2407.

Unknown – light engines/goods, LSW lines:- H1 2041 'Peveril Point'; K10 149; L11 414; L12 432; E1 1511; U1 1892.

On my way from Waterloo and back, I noted:- 'Lord Nelson' 853 'Sir Richard Grenville', 857 'Lord Howe', 862 'Lord Collingwood'; N15 448 'Sir Tristram', 750 'Morgan le Fay', 780 'Sir Persant', 793 'Sir Ontzlake'; H15 488,; S15 833; T14 446; H2 2425 'Trevose Head'; V 931 'King's Wimbledon'; L11 168; G6 160, 263, 354; M7 38.

I usually travelled from London to and from home, at my father's farm near Tewkesbury, the long way round by the LMS from Euston via Birmingham, because it was more interesting – and cost no more. On my journey of **11 September**

Class	Number	Working	Notes
M7	667	Empty stock?	
LMS 3F 0-6-0	3246 (Cricklewood)	Freight Feltham – WLER, Brent?	
O2	212	Carriage shunting	
Lord Nelson	855 'Robert Blake'	Bournemouth EP	
'700'	701	Freight, Nine Elms - Feltham?	
V	932 'Blundell's'	Basingstoke OP	
T14	459	Basingstoke OP	
M7	322	Empty stock?	
W	1919	WLER freight, Old Oak Common?	
LMS 3F 0-6-0T	7431 (Cricklewood)	WLER freight, ?Brent	
LNE(GN) N1 0-6-2T	4552 (Hornsey)	Freight Feltham – Ferme Park?	
Lord Nelson	857 'Lord Howe'	Bournemouth EP	
LMS 8F 2-8-0	8133 (Toton)	WLER freight, Brent?	
M7	241	Empty stock?	
'Merchant Navy'	21C8 'Orient Line'	West of England EP	
LMS 4F 0-6-0	4345 (Willesden)	WLER freight, Willesden	
I1X	2010	Victoria – Oxted line OP	
K&ESR 0-8-0T	949 'Hecate'	Carriage shunting	Unique loco, acquired from the K&ESR
L11	414	Freight, ?Nine Elms - Feltham	
K	2350	Freight, Brighton line	
LMS 4F 0-6-0	4349 (Willesden)	Freight Feltham – Willesden?	
I3	2027	Victoria – Oxted line OP	
N15	784 'Sir Nerovens'	West of England EP	15 coaches
LNE(GN) N1 0-6-2T	4582 (Hornsey)	Freight Feltham – Ferme Park?	
S15	505	?	
GW 57XX 0-6-0T	8760 (Old Oak Common)	?Feltham – South Lambeth freight	

TABLE 5: Clapham Junction, Tuesday 8 September 1942 (c. 11.00 – 12.30)

CONTINUED FROM SOUTHERN WAY No. 14 - April 2011.

References to footnotes in the text will be found on page 32.

Table 5 continued			
N15	771 'Sir Sagramore'	?Special	
M7	132	Empty stock	
LMS(LNW) 0-8-0	8893 (Willesden)	WLER freight, ?Willesden	
I3	2076	Victoria – Oxted line OP	
E6X	2407	Central Section freight	
V	928 'Stowe'	Basingstoke OP	
T14	443	?	
E1	1019	?	
H	1553	Vans?	
N	1810	Central Section freight	
H	1319	Vans?	
LMS Stanier Cl. 5 4-6-0	5240 (Willesden)	WLER freight, ?Willesden	
B4X	2052	Victoria – Oxted line OP?	
M7	38	Empty stock	
LNE(GE) J17	8175 (Cambridge)	WLER freight, ?Temple Mills	
LMS 3F 0-6-0	3800 (Cricklewood)	Brent freight?	
M7	33	Vans?	
W	1912	WLER freight	
B1	1455	?	Unusual
N15	448 'Sir Tristram'	West of England EP	

Top - Top – SR Maunsell S15 class 4-6-0 No. 834 outside Feltham Shed, 27 September 1947.

Bottom – Another 'Paddlebox', No. 459 on the turntable at Nine Elms Shed, 1 March 1947. The last of this rather unloved class was withdrawn in June 1951.

Opposite page - 'Described on the original print as The Fair Sex'. The locations are not recorded. The service badge worn the lapel of the porteress will be noted.

RCHS collection

1942 I noted at **Worcester (Shrub Hill)** SR No. 2091, one of the two I3 4-4-2Ts that the SR loaned to the GWR for about 12 months in 1942-43. I saw the other, No. 2089 at **Worcester** on **18 September**[19]. Then on **24 September** at **Ashchurch**, loaned SR K10 No. 137 (of Gloucester LMS) appeared on a pick-up Goods. On my return journey to school on **25 September** I noted several SR engines on the LMS and the S&D:- S11 396 (coupled to LMS 0-6-0 4422) at Hatherley Junction; K10 138 at Gloucester LMS Shed; K10 135 at Berkeley Road; S11 398 at Bath; T1 6 at Stalbridge.

At the end of the Autumn Term on **18 December 1942**, I travelled up to **Waterloo** from **Blandford** via **Bournemouth West**, noting:- T9 304 at Blandford (my train, 07.00 from Bath); LN 864 'Sir Martin Frobisher' and S11 400 at Poole; T6 681 at Parkstone; 'Lord Nelson' 851 'Sir Francis Drake' (on 10.20 to Waterloo, my train), V 928 'Stowe' and 933 'King's Canterbury', T9 288, M7 57, 254 and LMS 0-6-0 4557 at Bournemouth West; Q 543, L12 429, M7 112 at Bournemouth Central; 'Lord Nelson' 856 'Lord St Vincent', L11 410, M7 28 at Brockenhurst; 0-4-0T 77S at Redbridge; L11 172, L12 438 at Southampton Central; S15 845, D15 469 at Tunnel Junction; 'Lord Nelson' 862 'Lord Collingwood' at St Denys; T9 708, Q1 C3, Q 532, '700' 327, '0395' 3509, Z 952, G6 274, E1 2127, T1 364 at Eastleigh; T3 571, U 1633 at Wootton Box; S15 839, T9 307, U 1622/32/3, G6

348, M7 56 at Basingstoke; B4 2063 at Winchfield; H15 491, '700' 308 at Farnborough; N15 783 'Sir Gillemere' at Pirbright Junction; S15 832, K10 381, G6 262, 349, M7 43, 324 at Woking; U 1613/9 at Weybridge; '700' 309 at Walton-on-Thames; '700' 701 at Wimbledon; B1 1445, Q 541 at Clapham Junction; L 1761 at Pouparts Junction; V 929 'Malvern' at Nine Elms; H15 482, V 925 'Cheltenham' at Waterloo. No doubt I missed a lot else, but it was mid-winter.

In spite of the weather, I took my opportunities to watch trains during my two weeks in London over Christmas. On **20 December** I went to **Cricklewood**, where I saw S15 842 and '700' 693 on workings from Feltham. On **21 December** my mother took me from **Waterloo** to **Horsley** and back, to see her house. I noted:- 'Lord Nelson' 855 'Robert Blake', V 927 'Clifton' and 932 'Blundells', M7 38 at Waterloo; N15 804 'Sir Cador of Cornwall', H15 331, G6 353 at Nine Elms; N15 767 'Sir Valence', O2 212, M7 322, 667/73, H 1553 and LMS 0-6-0 4440 at Clapham Junction; K10 149, L11 154, '700' 692, C2X 2553, M7 123 at Wimbledon; H15 483 at Berrylands; K10 391 at Oxshott, then N15 449 'Sir Torre' at Wimbledon; D1 1739 at Clapham Junction; 'Lord Nelson' 850 'Lord Nelson', N15 780 'Sir Persant' at Nine Elms; 'Lord Nelson' 860 'Lord Hawke', M7 241 at Waterloo. On **24 December** I went – by bus – to **Clapham Junction**, where I stood for two hours and saw:-

7

'Merchant Navy' 21C8 'Orient Line', 21C10 'Blue Star', N15 777 'Sir Lamiel', 784 'Sir Nerovens', 785 'Sir Mador de la Porte', N15X 2333 'Remembrance', H15 486, S15 507, T14 460/2, H2 2422 'North Foreland', V 927 'Clifton', K10 391, L11 154, 414, L12 427/32, B4X 2072, U 1616/7, 1798, C 1722, C2X 2451, W 1914/20, I3 2084/6/90, 0-8-0T 949 'Hecate', O2 204, M7 33/8, 130, 249/51, 322, H 1005, 1552, R 1667; 'foreigners' were:- LMS 4-6-0 5411, 0-8-0 9021, 0-6-0 3246, 4438/40; LNE J15 7894, 7945, N1 4573/90, 4604 -- quite a remarkable selection. Returning to Waterloo by train, I saw:- D1 1145 and 'Merchant Navy' 21C7 'Aberdeen Commonwealth'. The engines seen at Clapham Junction would have been distributed between very much the same workings as listed before for the September observations.

On **4 January 1943** I went home to Tewkesbury, again via Birmingham, and saw I3 2091 again at **Worcester**. On this holiday the latest excitement was the appearance of the extraordinary-looking US Army S160 2-8-0s, at first on the GWR, then the LMS – but they did not work on the SR, although they must have passed over it on their way to the Continent late in 1944. When I went back to School on **22 January**, I noted loaned SR K10 389 at Gloucester and 137 at Bristol (Temple Meads), through which I again deviated my journey to Bath; on the S&D, S11 401 was my train engine from Bath to Blandford and I noted T9 303 at Templecombe, S11 399 at Stalbridge.

During the Spring Term I got sufficiently 'run down' from the annual 'flu' that I merited a week of recuperation up in London, staying with my mother. I made good use of it to watch trains – weather permitting. I travelled up on **27 February** to **Waterloo from Blandford via Templecombe**, noting:- S11 404 at Blandford (on 06.48 OP Bournemouth West - Bath, my train to Templecombe); T9 304 at Shillingstone (on 07.00 OP Bath – Bournemouth West); at Templecombe: 'Merchant Navy' 21C9 'Shaw Savill' (07.30 EP Exeter Central – Waterloo, as far as Salisbury, my train), N15 455 'Sir Launcelot', T1 3, 5 (shunting S&D); at Salisbury N15 450 'Sir Kay' (which took over my train), 451 'Sir Lamorak', 452 'Sir Meliagrance', S15 827/32/40, T9 122, 285, L12 425, Z 957, T1 361; A12 652 at Porton: K10 341, L12 423/6 at Andover Junction; 'Lord Nelson' 857 'Lord Howe' at Worting Junction; T9 311, 706, T3 563, U 1623, Q1 C19, '700' 368, also GW 4-6-0 6817 'Gwenddwr Grange' at Basingstoke; D1 1739 at Fleet; N15 741 'Joyous Gard', Q1 C8, E4 2500, M7 22 at Woking; K10 386 at Wimbledon; I3 2079 at Clapham Junction; 'Merchant Navy' 21C8 'Orient Line', H 1552 at Waterloo. Then on **2 March** I spent about 1½ hours at **Clapham Junction**, noting:- 'Merchant Navy' 21C8 'Orient Line', 'Lord Nelson' 857 'Lord Hood', 860 'Lord Hawke', 862 'Lord Collingwood', N15 452 'Sir Meliagrance', 753 'Melisande', 771 'Sir Sagramore', H15 491, S15 842, T14 445/61, V 924 'Haileybury', B4X 2073, U 1632, C2X 2448, I3 2026/81, W 1916/9/20, 0-8-0T 949 'Hecate', E6 2409, O2 179, M7 40, 130/2, 241/51, 319/22, 673, H 1548/53, R1 1667; also LMS 0-6-0 3246; LNE N1 4588. I returned to **Victoria** – where dance-music was being played over the PA system, noting:- E2 2105 at South Lambeth; N15 799 'Sir Ironside', H1 2038 'Portland Bill', H 1265, 1554 at Victoria. On **4 March** – accompanied by my mother! – I went round various South London stations looking for tickets, noting:- at Blackfriars *no* SR,

but LMS 2-6-2Ts 22, 28 and LNE N1 4551/62/5, J52 4258; at Walworth Road LNE J52 3926 – all in quite a short period, showing the intensity of MWL freight traffic. At Penge West C2X 2448; at New Cross Gate (mainly outside the Shed) H1 2038 'Portland Bill', K 2348, C2X 2535, I3 2084, W 1919, E6 2408/17, E1 2164; at Bricklayers Arms Junction V 918 'Hurstpierpoint', H 1326, 1500; U1 1894 at London Bridge; R1 1708 at Cannon Street.

On **5 March**, in 90 minutes at **West Hampstead**, where you could observe traffic on the ex-Midland, ex-North London and ex-GC lines all at the same time, I noted *35* locomotives, the following five SR passing on the North London:- B1 1450 + U1 1908, Q1 C22/9, C 1291. That afternoon I had reluctantly to return to School, catching the 14.50 from **Waterloo** and changing at **Templecombe** for **Blandford**; 'Merchant Navy' 21C10 'Blue Star' hauled me as far as Salisbury, then 21C2 'Union Castle' on to Templecombe; LMS 0-6-0 4466 to Blandford.

I noted the following:- At Waterloo:- N15 755 'The Red Knight', 782 'Sir Brian', V 928 'Stowe', T9 311, U 1619, M7 40, 667; '700' 701, 0-6-0T 756 'A.S. Harris', G6 353 at Nine Elms; H15 483 + K10 386 at Queens Road; 949 'Hecate', O2 179 at Clapham Junction; U 1615 at Malden; S15 501, K10 343, Q1 C30, M7 43, 58, 676 at Woking; V 929 'Malvern' at Brookwood; T14 445, M7 26 at Farnborough; S15 506, 836, V 930 'Radley', 933 'King's Canterbury', L11 405, L12 434, T9 314, U 1622/9, also GW 2-6-2T 6136 at Basingstoke; T9 707, U 1636, A12 598, also GW 2-6-0s 4326, 6326, and 2-6-2T 5563 at Andover Junction; A12 652 at Grateley; 'Merchant Navy' 21C9 'Shaw Savill', 'Lord Nelson' 858 'Lord Duncan', N15 773 'Sir Lavaine', H15 331/2, S15 840, T9 712/25, U 1632, M7 60, plus no less than six GW (4-6-0 5002 'Ludlow Castle', 5019 'Treago Castle', 2-8-0 3049, 2-6-0 6353, 2-8-0T 4260 and 0-6-0T 5781) at Salisbury; another GW was seen at Wilton - 4-6-0 6845 'Paviland Grange'; H15 475 at Dinton; L11 440 at Semley; U 1621 at Gillingham; N15 450 'Sir Kay', 786 'Sir Lionel', 792 'Sir Hervis de Revel', K10 152, U 1794 at Templecombe, also T9 304 and T1 4 on the S&D there.

On **2 April 1943**, I was off for the Easter Holidays, travelling to London from **Blandord** (on the 07.15 ex-Templecombe with T9 304) to **Bournemouth West**, then by the 10.20 to **Waterloo** behind 'Lord Nelson' 854 'Howard of Effingham'. On this journey I recorded just *one* LMS engine (0-6-0 4558 at Bournemouth West), most of the rest SR – but I probably missed a lot of numbers, especially at Eastleigh:- S11 398 at Blandford; K10 394 at Creekmoor Halt; L11 165, X6 659 at Poole; 'Lord Nelson' 861 'Lord Anson', S11 399 at Branksome; H15 521, V 927 'Clifton', T9 312, L12 438, M7 104 at Bournemouth West; K10 136 at Gas Works Junction; T3 571, '700' 695/6 at Brockenhurst; A12 598, T1 8 at Millbrook; T9 114 at Southampton Central; N15 743 'Lyonesse' at Tunnel Junction; G6 264 at Northam; S15 513 at St Denys; L12 419, D15 463, Q1 C14, '700' 317, '0395' 3101, 3397, A12 609, T1 20, 366 at Eastleigh; U 1633, '700' 350 at Micheldever; H15 523, V 933 'King's Canterbury', T9 726, U 1615, '700' 693, G6 278, M7 56, also GW 4-6-0 6812 'Chesford Grange' and 2-8-0 2831, at Basingstoke; V 930 'Radley' at Hook; S15 508, Q1 C8 at Farnborough; S15 833 at Brookwood;

L12 427, U 1800, G6 349, M7 43, 324 at Woking; '700' 699 at Weybridge; C2X 2437 at Wimbledon; H 1266 at Clapham Junction; 'Lord Nelson' 853 'Sir Richard Grenville', 863 'Lord Rodney', N15 778 'Sir Pelleas', T 1602 at Nine Elms; V 924 'Haileybury', U 1622 at Waterloo.

During the ensuing two weeks in London I did a lot of train-watching. I had another three spells of an hour or two at **West Hampstead**, seeing on the NLR:- SR Q1s C24/5 and C 1244 on **3 April**, Q1 C34 and C 1255 on **5 April**, then on **13 April** Q1s C22/4 and C 1059, 1255. As well, while watching the WLR on the bank between **North Pole and Mitre Bridge Junctions** along with all the GW workings at Old Oak East Junction, on **6 April** I saw:- B1 1443 + D1 1747 on a Special and on freight C 1715 and Ws 1921/5, on **9 April** W 1921 again, then on **11 April** at **Cricklewood** Q1s C21/5 again.

On **15 April 1943**, I travelled down to Ashchurch this time from Paddington via Gloucester and saw at **Reading (SR):-** S15 841, F1 1140, U 1611/27, N 1861, C 1692, and loaned K10 137 at **Gloucester**. K10 137 turned up again at **Ashchurch** while I was there on **23 April**, also S11 400 (of Bath), both working freight, and on **30 April** I saw K10 138 on a goods at **Lansdown Junction (Cheltenham)**. When I went back to school from **Ashchurch** – again via Bristol – **on 4 May**, I noted:- K10 138 at Gloucster (Barnwood) Shed and K10 137 at Charfield, while K10 388 was on Bristol (Barrow Road) Shed. On the – tedious – run on the 16.25 S&D train from **Bath**, which took until 18.55 to reach **Blandford**, I noted only two SR engines:- S11 404 at Bath; T1 3 at Stalbridge[20].

That summer I was old enough to be allowed to be more enterprising with excursions at week-ends, at least by bicycle – mine had no gears. On **16 May** I went to **Semley** *(Table 6)*, on the SR Salisbury – Exeter main line, where in 105 minutes I saw six trains (including two freights -- not bad for a Sunday), three of them hauled by novel Bulleid Pacifics:-

Blake', 858 'Lord Duncan', N15 777 'Sir Lamiel', 793 'Sir Ontzlake', T9 113, L12 424/9/30, Q 549; M7 106/7/12, O2 229, B4 99 at Bournemouth Central; M7 47, 51, 111/31 at Bournemouth West; S11 403 at Bailey Gate.

On **8 July** the School had a whole day's holiday -- to celebrate the birth of a child to one of the masters! – and I cycled with a friend to **Cole**, where we spent three hours watching trains where the S&D crossed the GW main West Country line near Bruton. The GWR was interesting and quite busy, but there were only three trains on the S&D and the only SR engines we noted were:- S11 402 (on the 09.10 Bournemouth West to Bath) at Cole; at Templecombe N15 456 'Sir Galahad' and S15 831 on the main line; S11 401 on the S&D. Then on **30 July** I went home for my Summer Holidays, *by bicycle* as far as Bristol, then train to **Ashchurch**: on the LMS I noted K10 388 at Charfield and 389 at Gloucester (both on goods).

With the great US Army Depot at **Ashchurch** now in full swing, traffic there was more intense and train-watching more rewarding than ever and I went there during **August 1943** whenever my father let me off working on the farm. However, the only observation of one of the loaned SR engines I made was of S11 400, going Down light-engine on 7 August. In September 1943 I was up in London for only a few days, but during 90 minutes at my favourite spot at Old Oak Common East on **6 September** I noted 10 workings on the WLR, which included three SR:- C 1245 on freight, and U 1639 and Q 535 on Specials. On **11 September** I spent 80 minutes in the afternoon at **Clapham Junction**, travelling to and from **Waterloo** and noting:- N15 452 'Sir Meliagrance', H15 521, D1 1247, M7 38, 123 at Waterloo; N15 767 'Sir Valence', N15X 2331 'Beattie' at Vauxhall; 'Lord Nelson' 852 'Sir Walter Raleigh', H15 478, 0-6-0T 756 'A.S. Harris', G6 266 at Nine Elms; C 1480 at Pouparts Junction; LNE N1 4552 at West London Junction. Then at **Clapham Junction**:- 'Lord Nelson' 857 'Lord Howe', 861 'Lord

TABLE 6: Semley, 16 May 1943		
Class	Number	Working
N15	453 'King Arthur'	09.50 Ilfracombe – Waterloo
'Merchant Navy'	21C9 'Shaw Savill'	11.00 Waterloo – Plymouth Friary
'Merchant Navy'	21C5 'Canadian Pacific'	09.43 Bude/09.53 Launceston/10.00 Plymouth Friary – Waterloo
N15	454 'Queen Guinevere'	11.45 Portsmouth & Southsea – Plymouth Friary
U	1635	13.40 OP Salisbury – Exeter, ?on to Plymouth
'Merchant Navy'	21C1 'Channel Packet'	Up freight
N15	790 'Sir Villiars'	Down freight

Two weeks later (30 May) I cycled all the way to Dorchester and then was fool enough to sit beside the GW line to Castle Cary and saw only three trains in two hours. At half-term I went to **Weymouth** (by bus) and stayed at a hotel with my mother. We went on excursions and I saw quite a few trains, but they were nearly all GW, except on **21 June** when we took a train to **Bournemouth Central** and later I returned to **Blandford via Bournemouth West**. SR locomotives observed were:- V 927 'Clifton' at Weymouth (11.30 OP to Bournemouth); K10 146; G6 162, O2 233 at Dorchester South; D15 472, '700' 695 at Wool; Q1 C11, M7 21 at Wareham; L11 148, B4 100 at Hamworthy Junction; T9 307, M7 50 at Poole; 'Lord Nelson' 853 'Sir Richard Grenville', 854 'Howard of Effingham', 855 'Robert

Anson', N15 455 'Sir Launcelot', 752 'Linette', 755 'The Red Knight', 772 'Sir Percivale', 775 'Sir Agravaine', 788 'Sir Urre of the Mount', T14 461, V 903 'Charterhouse', L12 416, T9 305, D 1734, B4X 2045, N 1844, U1 1902, '700' 339, 692, C 1297, G6 257, M7 31, 40, 130, 249, 318, 673; O2 204/12, H 1266, 1544/53. On return:- N15 787 'Sir Menadeuke', K10 149 at Queens Road; G6 264 at Nine Elms; 'Lord Nelson' 859 'Lord Hood' at Waterloo.

On going back to School from **Ashchurch via Bath** on **24 September**, I noted just the following SR:- K10 138 at Charfield; T1 1 at Evercreech Junction; K10 344 at Templecombe; S11 402 at Sturminster Newton. On a run from **Blandford** to **Bournemouth West** and back on **6 November**

1943:- S11 399 at Spetisbury; T9 706, L12 425 at Poole; N15 751 'Etarre', L12 428 at Bournemouth West; T9 286, 719, '700' 700, M7 318 at Poole. Returning home to Ashchurch on **17 December 1943**, I saw just:- S11 399 at Blandford; K10 388 at Wickwar. Ashchurch was as fascinating as ever in the Christmas Holidays, but I noted none of the loaned SR engines. Nor did I on my journey up to Euston on 4 January 1944 – on which I deviated further by going round via Nuneaton, to see the tremendous traffic in the Washwood Heath area[21]. During a short sojourn in London in **January 1944**, before I had to go back to School I was able to visit my favourite haunts. On **7 January** in 75 minutes at **West Hampstead**, of 32 engines I saw three were SR – all on the North London line on freight:- Q1 C37, C 1059/90. In a short spell at **Old Oak Common East** on **10 January** I noted:- N 1872, C 1287 and W 1920 on the WLER. On **14 January** I went down from **Charing Cross** to **Chislehurst**, where I discovered a secluded spot next to where the ex-SER main line crossed the ex-LC&D line and from where you could see as well almost everything on the loops that interconnected these routes – except the Up SER –> LC&D curve, which was taken by Boat Expresses to Victoria. There I watched trains for 2½ hours and saw 19 steam workings. On the way there I noted:- V 935 'Sevenoaks' at Charing Cross; V 903 'Charterhouse', B4X 2067 at London Bridge; I3 2030/89, H 1324 at North Kent East Junction; N15 802 'Sir Durnore', L 1769, C 1480, 1715; W 1935, Z 950/1/6 at Hither Green; V 921 'Shrewsbury', C 1090 at Grove Park; V 936 'Cranleigh' at Chislehurst, *(Table 7)*.

On the return journey:- C 1277 at Grove Park; F1 1249, B1 1459, N 1818, W 1919/22, LMS 0-6-0T 7244, LNE N1 4573 at Hither Green; C 1582 at Parks Bridge Junction; V 915 'Brighton' at London Bridge; V 917 'Ardingly' at Charing Cross.

On **20 January 1944** I had to go back to School, travelling from **Waterloo via Bournemeouth West to Blandford**:- H15 476, V 927 'Clifton' (13.30 to Bournemouth, my train), T9 726, M7 123 at Waterloo; H15 490, M7 319 at Nine Elms; LMS 2-6-2T 30 at West London Junction; N15X 2331 'Beattie', H15 489, M7 32/8, H 1553 at Clapham Junction; L11 156, 411, M7 673 at Wimbledon; H16 520 at Hampton Court Junction; 'Lord Nelson' 854 'Howard of Effingham' at Esher; F1 1042 at Walton-on-Thames; M7 328 at Weybridge; N15 777 'Sir Lamiel', H15 484, K10 381, M7 26, 676 at Woking; H15 474 at Brookwood; T9 704 at Winchfield; D1 1492 at Hook; N15 785 'Sir Mador de la Porte', H15 487, S15 512, T14 459, T9 708, L11 407, L12 426, U 1633, Q1 C22, G6 265, 348 at Basingstoke; Q1 C24 at Winchester; S15 496, 843, K10 138[22], 342, G6 261, E1 2138/47 at Eastleigh; G6 267 at St Denys; N15 743 'Lyonesse', S15 842, D15 469 at Southampton Central; L11 148 at Millbrook; N15 774 'Sir Gaheris', T14 460 at Lyndhurst Road; L12 415, M7 28, 107 at Brockenhurst; K10 136 at Christchurch; K10 146, T9 304, 728, M7 112/31, O2 229 at Bournemouth Central; 'Lord Nelson' 856 'Lord St Vincent', L12 420, M7 111, LMS 0-6-0 4402 (17.15 to Bath, my train to Blandford) at Bournemouth West; M7 59 at Branksome; L11 410, M7 106 at Poole.

Salisbury was a particularly interesting station, with so much special wartime traffic being worked through there off the GWR. I managed a three-hour spell at half-term on **26 February 1944 (Table 8).**

TABLE 7: Chislehurst / Bickley 14 January 1944			
Class	Number	Working	Notes
V	937 'Epsom'	?07.03 EP Margate – Canterbury – Ashford – Cannon St.	
C	1257	Up light engine, SER line	
R1	1710	Up light engine, LCDR line	
V	920 'Rugby'	?07.30 Margate – Dover – Charing Cross	
C	1268	Down Goods, SER line	
N15	765 'Sir Gareth'	?10.35 Victoria – Ramsgate	
N15	799 'Sir Ironside'	?08.40 Ramsgate/09.00 Dover - Victoria	
N15	783 'Sir Gillemere'	?11.15 Charing Cross – Deal	
N	1874	Down freight, LCDR	
V	908 'Westminster'	?09.45 Ramsgate - Victoria	
C	1293	Down goods, LCDR line	
(C	1715)	Down (new empty) US Army box-cars, SER line	Operation 'FORTITUDE'?
N1	1878	Up freight, LCDR to SER line	
V	901 ''Winchester'	?12.25 Charing Cross – Tonbridge - Ashford	
N15	796 'Sir Dodinas le Savage'	?12.35 Victoria – Ramsgate	
D	1738	Up light engine, LCDR line	
C	1724	Up goods, LCDR line	
V	931 'King's Wimbledon'	?12.29 Tonbridge – Charing Cross	
C	1271	Down freight, SER - LCDR	

TABLE 8: Salisbury, Saturday 26 February 1944				
Time, approx	Class	Number	Working	Notes
10.10	Z	957	Shunting	
	'Merchant Navy'	21C7 'Aberdeen Commonwealth'	07.30 Exeter – Waterloo	
	H15	483	Light Engine	
	H15 + K10	478 + 382	Light Engines coupled	
	Q	530	Up mineral	Probably stone from Meldon?
	'Merchant Navy'	21C2 'Union Castle'	09.16 OP ex-Templecombe, then to Shed	
	N15	770 'Sir Prianius'	Down empties to Depot	?Military Depot?

Table 8 continued				
	GW 57XX 0-6-0T	Shunting		
	H15	489	?07.24 OP ex-Waterloo, then to Shed	Returned to work 11.55 OP to Waterloo
	H15 + S15	476 + 827	Light Engines coupled	
	M7	41	Pilot	
	M7	60	Pilot	
	S15	825	?Relief to Exeter, ahead of 09.00 ex-Waterloo	Surmise!
	L12	421	Off, 08.55 EP Portsmouth & Southsea – Cardiff	
	GW 'Hall'	4916 'Crumlin Hall'	Off, 08.12 Bristol Temple Meads – Portsmouth & Southsea	Returned with freight, see below
	'Merchant Navy'	21C8 'Orient Line'	Off Shed, onto 09.00 EP Waterloo - Exeter	
11.00	T9 + U	118 + 1637	Light Engines coupled	
	GW 'Grange'	6845 'Paviland Grange'	On to 08.12 ex-Portsmouth	
	'Lord Nelson'	857 'Lord Howe'	Off, 09.00 EP Waterloo - Exeter	
	GW 'Hall' + '2883' 2-8-0	(4916 'Crumlin Hall') + 3866	Down freight from Yard	4916 must have just given train a start, as it later worked 12.25 to Bristol (below)
	GW 43XX 2-6-0	5306	Transfer freight	
	T9 + T9	285 + 288	Up 3-coach Special	Undoubtedly VIPs!
	'0395'	3441	Shunting	
	Q1	C16	Light Engine	
	T1 + N15	361 + 776 'Sir Galagars'	Light Engines coupled	
	V	932 'Blundells'	09.30 OP ex-Waterloo	
	GW 28XX 2-8-0	2811	Up mineral to Romsey line	Working through onto SR
	H15	331	Light Engine	
12.00	T9	303	11.55 OP to Waterloo	
	D15	464	Off, 10.32 Portsmouth & Southsea – Bristol Temple Meads	
	GW 'Hall'	(4916 'Crumlin Hall')	Onto 10.32 Portsmouth & Southsea – Bristol Temple Meads	
	T9 + M7	727 + 675	Light Engines coupled	
	'Merchant Navy'	21C4 'Cunard White Star'	08.15 Torrington/Ilfracombe - Waterloo	Loaded to 16 coaches
	Unidentified	--	10.50 Waterloo – Ilfracombe/Torrington	
	GW 28XX 2-8-0	2802	Up freight (timber) to Dunbridge	Working through onto SR
	N15	449 'Sir Torre'	10.59 Waterloo – Plymouth/Padstow	
	A12	654	Light Engine	
	G6	237	Light Engine	
13.15	U	1790	12.24 OP Templecombe - Waterloo	

Entering Basingstoke with a Down goods on 4 June 1949 is LSW Drummond T9 class 4-4-0 No. 288.

WARTIME SOUTHERN Part 3

At the end of that term on **31 March 1944**, I travelled back to **Waterloo via Bournemouth West,** *(Table 9)* noting, in spite of people in the corridor blocking my view to the left, quite a good sample of what was moving – including WD 2-8-0 'Austerities' now on the SR and even more SR 4-4-0s shunting yards all along the route. What I noted down is interesting, but there's no doubt I missed much.

Location	Class	Number	Working	Notes
TABLE 9: Blandford - Bournemouth West / Central - Waterloo 31 March 1944				
Blandford, 08.12	S11	402	07.15 OP Templecombe – Bournemouth West	My train
Poole	'Lord Nelson'	855 'Robert Blake'	Up empty wagons!!	Unusual – even in wartime
	L11	169	Shunting	
Parkstone	'Lord Nelson'	854 'Howard of Effingham'	Down EP?	
Branksome	S11	403	091.0 OP Bournemouth West – Bath	
B'mouth West, 09.15 – 10.20	'Lord Nelson'	856 'Lord St Vincent'	10.20 EP to Waterloo	My train
	LMS 4-4-0	696	On Shed	
	M7	318	Carriage shunting	
	M7	47	Shunting	
	T9	122	Empty stock	
	D15	467	07.46 OP from Eastleigh	
B'mouth Central, c. 10.30	'700'	315	Down goods	
	Q	548	Light engine	
	G6	239	Shunting	
Sway	**WD 2-8-0**	7440	Down freight	Noteworthy
Brockenhurst	K10	135	Shunting	
	M7	111	Lymington OP	
Beaulieu Road	L11	161	Shunting WD Siding	
Lyndhurst Road	'Lord Nelson'	864 'Sir Martin Frobisher'	08.30 EP Waterloo - Weymouth	
Totton	'700'	317	Fawley branch freight	
Redbridge	'700'	308	Down goods	
Millbrook	L12	425	Down EP, ?10.32 Portsmouth & S. – Bristol T.M.	
	Q	534	Shunting	
	GW 2-6-0	6326	Light engine	
So'ton Central, c. 11.20	T9	114	?10.45 OP from Micheldever	
	D15	472	Light engine	
	WD 2-8-0	7439	Down freight	Noteworthy
Northam Yard	G6	274	Shunting	
St Denys	A12	627	Shunting	
Swaythling	'Lord Nelson'	861 'Lord Anson'	09.30 EP Waterloo – Bournemouth West	
Eastleigh	X6	666	Outside Works	?Withdrawn
	T9; D15; K; Q1	313; 471; 2349; C31	On Shed	
	K10	387	OP to Portsmouth	
	N15	768 'Sir Balin'	Down freight	
	T14; '0395'; G6	461; 3083; 261	Yard/Shunting	
St Cross Box	T14	443	Down OP	
Micheldever	U	1622	Shunting	
Basingstoke	H15; U; M7	330; 1627; 127, 248	On Shed	
Hook	V	931 'King's Wimbledon'	?10.54 OP Waterloo – Salisbury	
Winchfield	L12	418	Shunting	
	N15	785 'Sir Mador de la Porte'	Down freight	
Fleet	A12	643	Shunting	
Pirbright Junction	N15	776 'Sir Galagars'	Down EP	
	S15	513	Down freight	
Brookwood	Q1	C4	Down freight	
Woking	S15	512	Down freight	
	S15	836	Down freight to Portsmouth line	
	H15; N; G6; M7	488; 1873; 349; 43, 324	In yard, shunting etc.	
West Weybridge	L12	416	Down freight	
Weybridge	'700'	699	Local goods	
Walton-on-Thames	L12	427	Shunting	
Hampton Court Junction	L11	154	Oxshott branch goods	
Wimbledon	K10; C2; E4X	391; 2535; 2489	Yard/shunting	
Clapham Junction	'Lord Nelson'	857 'Lord Howe'	Down *freight*	Noteworthy
	Q	540	Freight	
Nine Elms	N15; V	774 'Sir Gaheris'; 924 'Haileybury'	Light engines	
Waterloo	R1	1698	Pilot	

Top right - – 0-6-0T No. 756 'A.S. Harris' again, now working at Stewarts Lane as shed pilot, 7 April 1951.

Centre left – One of three surviving LB&SC R.J. Billinton C2 class 0-6-0s, No. 2436, at Three Bridges Shed, 11 December 1948.

Centre right – Two of the SE Stirling R1 class 0-6-0Ts, Nos. 1069 and 1147, modified with cut down cab and chimney for working on the Canterbury & Whitstable line, shunting engines at Ashford Shed on 6 July 1946; behind them is LB&SC C2X class 0-6-0 No. 2541 fresh from repair at the Works.

Bottom – LSW Drummond K10 class 4-4-0 No. 139 at Feltham Shed, 27 September 1947.

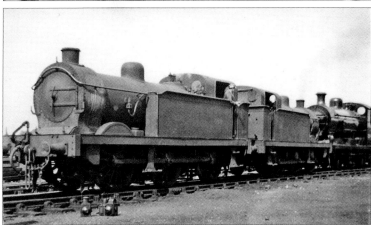

I then travelled down to Horsley (on the Waterloo – Guildford via Cobham line), where I stayed for 10 days and got around quite a bit mainly by bicycle, seeing a little of the frenetic build-up in advance of D-Day – not only on the railways but, for example, ammunition stacked up beside the roads through the Surrey woods. This was at the height of the final influx of US Forces (Operation BOLERO) and the accumulation of American and British Armies in the South of England. At that time, across the country up to 100 Special Troop trains per day (plus associated empty stock workings) and a similar number of Special Stores trains were being run.

TABLE 10: Guildford 2 April 1944

Class	Number	Working	Notes
U	1806	Up freight	
U	1628	Up Special	
U1	1891	OP to Redhill	
U	1627	OP from Reading	Returned later
A12	634	Goods	
Q	532	Light engine	
D3	2384	Horsham OP	
'700'	325	Light engine	
D	1729	OP from Reading	
U1	1892	Newcastle – Ashford EP	
Q1	C4	Light engine	
D3	2366	Horsham OP	
U1	1904	OP to Reading	

Right - SE&C Wainwright R1 class 0-4-4T No. 1706 on pilot duty at London Bridge (Low Level), 10 March 1948.
Bottom – LB&SC R.J. Billinton D3/M class (motor-fitted) 0-4-4T No. 2380 at Ashford Shed, 8 July 1946.

On **1 April**, going down from **Waterloo**, I noted:- N15 784 'Sir Nerovens' (on Up EP), V 925 'Cheltenham' + 931 'King's Wimbledon' at Vauxhall (Up light engines coupled); '700' 692, R1 1698 at Nine Elms; at Clapham Junction, T9 288 + U 1801 (on Up Special), G6 263, O2 179, M7 249, 318 and H 1553 (carriage shunting etc.); K10 149, 381 at Wimbledon (shunting). At Horsley, only the local goods was of interest: on 2 April – a *Sunday* - it had N 1873, on 3 April U 1619. That day I travelled into **Guildford** and in an hour or so I saw 13 engines at work *(Table 10):* in addition, the following were on Shed or shunting:- L11 154; T9 726; U1 1900; Q1 C17/22; G6 269; M7 246, 378.

On **4 April** I cycled via Dorking to **Redhill**. I noted U 1610 on an OP at Dorking Town and N 1873 on a freight at Betchworth: at Redhill during six hours *(Table 11):* it was fascinating.

Thus at **Redhill** in about four hours there were 18 freight trains. These were mainly on the Reading line, which was such an important link in the War, from 'Dunkirk' onwards. (They could certainly have done with a direct connection with the Tonbridge line, but it would have taken too long to build). In between all this freight traffic at Redhill were of course numerous electric trains, including those occupying the Reading line to Reigate.

I came back to Guildford by train, noting:- N 1813 (on OP to Redhill) at Betchworth; U1 1892 (on Newcastle – Ashford EP) at Chilworth; E4 2500 shunting at Shalford. Then in 30 minutes or so at **Guildford** before continuing to Horsley I noted (including some at the Shed):- K10 386, T9 726, U 1626, Q1 C22/36, Q 530/9, '700' 350, '0395' 3436, A12 622/38, G6 268/9/70, 349, M7 378, D3 2366. On **5 April** I noted:- '700s' 692 at Bookham and 701 (on an Up parcels) at Epsom.

SR Maunsell N15 'King Arthur' class 4-6-0 No. 774 'Sir Gaheris' is approaching Vauxhall on the 16.30 Waterloo to Bournemouth West, 24 April 1948.

TABLE 11: Redhill, Tuesday April 4 1944				
Time	Class	Number	Working	Notes
12.10	I1X	2595	On Shed	
	C2	2526	Shunting	
12.29	D	1730	11.38 OP ex-Tonbridge	Returned 17.10
12.35	U	1620	12.31 OP to Reading	
12.37	E4	2577	Up Goods and shunting	
12.41	Q1	C2	Freight to Reading line	
12.45 – 13.33	'Austerity'	WD 7434	Down freight, Brighton line	WD loco on loan to SR
12.49	Q1	C3	Mineral (stone) from Reading line	
13.05	U1	1900	Special from Tonbridge line	
13.14	B4X	2043	Took 1900's train onto Down Brighton line	
13.10	L12	422	11.05 OP ex-Reading	Returned on 15.10 OP to Reading
	D3	2367	Carriage-shunting	
13.20	E4	2507	Light Engine	
	I1X	2009	Carriage-shunting	
13.30	H	1518	OP from Tonbridge	Returned on 16.16 OP to Maidstone West
13.35	N + U	1407 + 1628	Freight from Reading line	
13.38	N	18.15	13.35 OP to Reading	
13.43	U1	1891	Freight to Reading line	
13.52	O1	1041	Down Goods, Brighton line	
14.08	O1	1109	Up Goods, Brighton line	
14.12	U1	1896	12.17 OP from Reading	Returned on 18.06 OP
14.20	D3	2374	14.09 OP to Tonbridge	
14.40	L	1765	Down Parcels, Brighton line	
	E4	2558	Shunting	
14.52	D1	1736	Unadvertised OP (?Special) from Reading line	Later worked 18.07 OP to Tonbridge
15.40	C2X	2545	Light Engine	
15.40	Q	537	Up Special freight, from Tonbridge line	
15.42	U1	1898	Freight from Reading line	
15.42	I1X	2008	OP to Reading line	
15.49	U1	1894	Goods from Reading line	
16.00	U	1806	13.50 OP ex-Reading	
16.21	Q	531	Freight from Reading line	Loco with Lemaître chimney
16.29	Q	536	Freight to Reading line	
16.41	U	1809	Freight from Reading line	
16.49	U	1610	14.50 OP ex-Reading	
16.57	D	1586	16.10 OP ex-Tonbridge	
17.19	U	1628	Freight to Reading line	
17.32	Q	538	Light Engine from Tonbridge line	
17.35	U	1804	16.42 OP ex-Guildford	
17.44	I1X	2006	17.36 OP to Reading	
17.49	C2X	2441	Freight from Reading line	
18.02	O1	(1041)	Goods from Reading line	

TABLE 12 Woking, Thursday April 6 1944

Time	Class	Number	Working	Notes
11.57	Q1	C3	Up freight	
11.58	N15	766 'Sir Geraint'	Up EP, 08.35 Bournemouth West - Waterloo	23 min. late
--	M7	43	Shunting	
--	M7	254	Station pilot	
12.04	Lord Nelson	858 'Lord Duncan'	Down EP, 11.30 Waterloo – Bournemouth West	
12.29	S15	514	Down freight	
12.36	S15	842	Up empties	
12.37	S15	515	Down Light Engine	
12.52	H15	490	Up freight	
- 12.54	Lord Nelson	861 'Lord Anson'	Up EP, 10.20 Bournemouth West - Waterloo	28 min. late
12.58	H15	524	Down freight	
- 12.59	L12	434	Up OP, 12.02 Basingstoke – Waterloo	
13.20	L12	416	Down freight	
13.26	'Austerity' 2-8-0	WD 7489	Up freight	WD loco on loan to SR
13.34 -	V	933 'King's Canterbury'	Down OP, 12.54 Waterloo – Basingstoke	
13.43	N15	770 'Sir Prianius'	Up Special freight[23]	
13.56	N15	773 'Sir Lavaine'	Up EP, ?08.29 Plymouth (Friary) – Waterloo	
13.57	N15X	2332 'StroudLey'	Down EP – Relief?	
13.58	Q1	C16	Up freight	
- 14.03	Lord Nelson	852 'Sir Walter RaLeigh'	Up EP, 11.00 Bournemouth West – Waterloo	
14.05 -	Lord Nelson	855 'Robert Blake'	Down EP, 13.30 Waterloo – Bournemouth West	
14.07	'Austerity' 2-8-0	WD 7491	Up Light Engine	WD loco on loan to SR
- 14.07	N15	771 'Sir Sagramore'	Up EP, ?Relief	
14.10	N15	785 'Sir Mador de la Porte'	Up Special freight	
- 14.20	T14	462	Up OP, 11.55 Salisbury – Waterloo	20 min. late
- 14.28	Lord Nelson	862 'Lord Collingwood'	Up Special	
14.25	N15	752 'Linette'	Up freight	
14.30	N15X	2333 'Remembrance'	Up Special freight	
- 14.31	N15	746 'Pendragon'	Down OP, 13.54 Waterloo – Basingstoke	
14.38	U	1800	Down freight	
14.48	H15	483	Up Special freight	
14.56	Q1	C7	Up empties	
15.01	M7	481	Local freight	
15.13	'Austerity' 2-8-0	WD 7493	Up empties	WD loco on loan to SR
15.17	T9	713	Up Light Engine	
15.23	N15	776 'Sir Galagars'	Down EP, 14.50 Waterloo –Ilfracombe/ Torrington/Plymouth (Friary)/Bude/Launceston	Extent of multi-portioning uncertain
- 15.31	N15	741 'Joyous Gard'	Down Relief EP to West of England	
15.37	Q1	C27	Down Light Engine	
15.38	Q1	C12	Up Special freight	
15.39	(T9	713)	Down Special empty stock	
15.55	V	929 'Malvern'	Up OP ?12.24 Templecombe – Waterloo	7 min. late
16.09	(N15	766 'Sir Geraint'	Down EP, 15.30 Waterloo – Bournemouth West	
16.15 -	N15	767 'Sir Valence'	Down EP, 15.30 Waterloo – Bournemouth West, 2nd part	
16.25	H15	488	Down Special	
16.22	Lord Nelson	857 'Lord Howe'	Up EP, 12.10 Bournemouth West – Waterloo	32 min. late
16.25	H15	474	Up empties	
16.29 -	Lord Nelson	854 'Howard of Effingham'	Up EP, 12.10 Bournemouth West – Waterloo, 2nd part	39 min. late
16.29	Q1	C20	Down Light Engine	
16.37	'700'	352	Down freight	
16.46 -	Lord Nelson	860 'Lord Hawke'	Up EP, ?Bournemouth West – Waterloo, 3rd part	28 min. late
16.48 -	T14	444	Down Relief OP	
16.51 -	V	928 'Stowe'	Up EP, ?Relief from?	24 min. late
16.55 -	D1	1492	Up Special OP	
16.56 -	Lord Nelson	863 'Lord Rodney'	Up EP, ?Relief from?	19 min. late
16.57	'Austerity' 2-8-0	WD 7497	Down freight	WD loco on loan to SR
16.58	N15X	2331 'Beattie'	Down Milk empties	
17.07	Lord Nelson	(852 'Sir Walter Raleigh')	Down EP, 16.35 Waterloo – Bournemouth West	
17.12	L12	427	Up OP, 16.16 Basingstoke - Waterloo	15 min. late
17.28	S15	499	Down freight	
17.35	N15	454 'Queen Guinevere'	Down OP, 17.00 Waterloo – Yeovil Junction	
17.40	U	1622	Up parcels	
1743-	U	1616	Down OP, 17.09 Waterloo – Basingstoke	
17.55	U	1803	Up freight	

On **6 April** I cycled to **Woking**, where I spent a most memorable six hours on the station *(Table 12)*. My day at Woking had been fascinating. Perhaps it was not surprising in the circumstances that I saw *22* freight trains in six hours that day. The LSW main line was not much of a freight artery anyway and normally most of the freight was run during the night -- there were too many passenger trains, especially electric trains, albeit the route was not electrified in those days beyond Pirbright Junction.

On the way back home, I noted at **Byfleet** in about 30 minutes:- 'Lord Nelson' 856 'Lord St Vincent', N15 775 'Sir Agravaine', 777 'Sir Lamiel' all on Up EP ruing about 20 minutes late, also H16 tank 517 on another Up freight. On **8 April** during cycling round I noted:- 'Lord Nelson' 855 'Robert Blake', M7 56 at Weybridge; at Sunbury T14 443 – surprisingly,

'700' 352; at Feltham Yard Q1 C16, '0395' 3163, G16 492 – and GW 4-6-0 6952 'Kimberley Hall'. Next – of all things – at Teddington I noted WD 2-8-0 7497 on Down empties[24]. Finally, about 20 minutes at Esher produced:- T9 718 and M7 319 light engines, T14 446 on Down EP, 'Lord Nelson' 856 'Lord St Vincent' on Up EP and N15X 2331 'Beattie' on Down Milk empties. On **9 April** (a Sunday) I noted the following at **Guildford** – mainly on Shed:- K10 141, 343, T9 311, L12 428/33, U 1799, 1802, Q1 C2, C3, C21, Q 533/45, '700' 698, '0395' 3436, A12 615/30/43, G6 268, M7 110/27, 324/78, 672. On **10 April**, I noted at **Surbiton**, incidently:- 'Lord Nelson' 851 'Sir Francis Drake', N15X 2330 'Cudworth', K10 149, L11 411, H16 518. On **11 April**, *(Table 13)* on returning from **Horsley to Waterloo**:-

TABLE 13: Horsley to Waterloo 11 April 1944				
Location	Class	Number	Working	Notes
Horsley 10.40	'700'	701	Shunting	
Hampton Court Junction	'Lord Nelson'	865'Sir John Hawkins'	Down EP	
Surbiton	**WD 2-8-0**	7436		Noteworthy
	V	932 'Blundells'	Down EP	
	U	1618	Up empty flats	For Army tanks etc.
	H15; K10; U; '700	484; 391; 1617; 694	In yard etc.	!!
Wimbledon	L11	411	In yard	
	U	1615	Down freight	
Clapham Junction	LMS 0-6-0	4384	Shunting Falcon Lane Goods	

SR Maunsell V class 'Schools' 4-4-0 No. 911 'Dover' charges out of Victoria past the East Box on the 16.05 to Ramsgate (made up of elderly SE&C stock, 17 July 1948.

Location	Class	Number	Working	Notes
Charing Cross	V; L1	912 'Downside'; 1755/9	Passenger	
Wandsworth Road	H	1554		
Nine Elms	'Lord Nelson'; N15; H15; L12; Q1; O2	856 'Lord St Vincent'; 770 'Sir Prianius', 773 'Sir Lavaine'; 483; 434; C31; 212	On Shed	
	D	1731	Up freight	Noteworthy
	V	931 'King's Wimbledon'	Up express	
	G6	160	Shunting	
	T14	444	Down EP	
Stewarts Lane, SE&C	D1	1749	Light engine	
	LMS 0-6-2T	7699	Parcels	
	N15	778 'Sir Pelleas'	Empty stock	
	N15	769 'Sir Balan'	Empty stock	
	H	1263	Shunting	
	B4	2042	Light engine	
	O1	1434	Light engine	
	I3	2083	Empty stock	
	WD 2-8-0	7433	Empty flat wagons	Noteworthy
	GW 0-6-0T	3736	Freight	
	E2	2107	Light engine	
	C	1718	Light engine	
Simultaneously:- Queens Road, LSW	U	1619	Empty stock	
	'Lord Nelson'	865 'Sir John Hawkins'	Up EP	
	M7	132	Empty stock	
	H	1553	Empty stock	
	N15	788 'Sir Urre of the Mount'	Up EP	
	Q1	C18	Up freight	
	M7	319	Empty stock	
	'700'	699	Light engine	
	H	1544	Empty stock	
Clapham Junction, c. 17.00 – 18.00	V; M7; H	931 'King's Wimbledon'; 123, 249/54/7, 673, 1544	Empty stock, etc., LSW	
	N15X	2333 'Remembrance'	Down parcels, LSW	
	J1	2325	Down Oxted OP, LBSC	
	(L12	434)	Down OP, LSW	
	R	1661	Kensington OP, WLER	
	I3	2029	Up Oxted OP, LBSC	
	LNE N1	4552	Light engine from WL	Probably to WLER
	'Lord Nelson'	861 'Lord Anson'	Up EP, LSW	
	O1	1380	Freight to WL	
	LMS 8F 2-8-0	8655	Empties, LBSCR to WLER	
	L11	155	Light engine to WL	
	I3	2086	Down Oxted OP, LBSC	
	U	1618	Special, WL to WLER	LMS coaches, ? Troops
	(N15	770 'Sir Prianius'	Down EP, LSW	
	U1	1905	Up freight, LBSC	
	N15	448 'Sir Tristram'	Up EP, LSW	
	U	1615	Light engine, LSW	
Battersea Wharf	U1	1909	Freight	
	E2	2102	Shunting	
Victoria	(N15	778 'Sir Pelleas'	Down EP, SECR	
	N15	782 'Sir Brian'		

The crowded train prevented me from seeing more, but even the above was representative of what was happening.

On **12 April**, with a friend I noted the following SR, mainly without taking a train: my diary account explains:- "We caught a tram from the Embankment to Nine Elms. There we found Stewarts Road blocked by street-fighters [i.e. infantry practising] and had to go a long way round to get to the spot for watching stuff coming out of Stewarts Lane Shed [i.e. where the Waterloo line was also visible]. We stayed there at least an hour, but didn't see very much. I later wandered [on my own] by Queens Road into Wandsworth Road and got a tram to Clapham Junction. There I stayed an hour. I took electric set numbers, which kept me busy in the rush-hour. I saw a nice few steam locos too. The I took an electric to Victoria and came home by 38 bus."

I logged the following steam locomotives (Table 14) -

The amount of freight (and the Specials) moving, even during the rush-hour, was noteworthy.

On **14 April**, I spent 11.45 – 13.15 at **East Croydon** (Table 15), noting in my diary that "I was amazed to see more steam trains than electric". [I did record 'Juice-Box' numbers at this time, but they are not reproduced here.]

That afternoon (15.10 – 18.00) at **West Hampstead**, SR engines seen on the North London line were:- '700' 350 and C 1090, 1572 – all on freight trains[25].

TABLE 15: East Croydon - Victoria 14 April 1944				
Location	Class	Number	Working	Notes
East Croydon, 11.45	E4	2479	Pilot	
	E4	2506	Shunting	
	U1	1903	Up Special	Presumably Troops
	K	2349	Down freight	
	I1X	2602	10.52 OP Tunbridge Wells West – Victoria	
	B4	2054	09.50 Eastbourne/10.18 Brighton – Oxted – Victoria	
	K	2351	Light engine	
	C2X	2446	Down freight	
	H2	2426 'St Alban's Head'	12.03 Victoria – Oxted – Brighton	
	K	2348	Up goods	
	E4	2516	Down goods	
	I1X	2008	Up parcels	
	U1	1909	Down Special	Presumably Troops
	E6X	2407	Up freight	
	U1	1897	Up empties	
	H2	2424 'Beachy Head'	10.50 Brighton – Oxted – Victoria	
	C2X	2544	Down freight	
13.15	C2X	2551	Down Special empties	Military
Norwood Yard	K; E3	2344; 2167, 2457	In yard	
Norwood Shed	E4	2472, 2562	On Shed	
	E4	2476/93	Light engines coupled	
New Cross Gate	H1; '700'; I3; D1	2038 'Portland Bill'; 326; 2028; 2235	On Shed	
	LNE F5 2-4-2T	7145		Off East London line

Abandoned with many other engines on the Dump at Eastleigh is LSW Adams A12 class 0-4-2 No. 555, 11 July 1946.

On **15 April** I travelled -- once again from Euston via Birmingham – down to **Ashchurch**. It was a Saturday, but freight traffic was still very heavy: on the way out of Birmingham there were *nine* freights queueing on the Up Goods lines between Kings Norton and Barnt Green, one of which with S11 396 (of Saltley) piloting a 4F 0-6-0; when I got to Ashchurch, K10 139 came light engine from Tewkesbury. In the ensuing two weeks or so I found the traffic on the Birmingham – Bristol main line enthralling, with many GW engines turning up at Ashchurch, also the new WD 2-10-0s as well as the 'Yanks' (S160 2-8-0s) and many other excitements there and at Gloucester and Cheltenham. However, I saw no more loaned SR locomotives until my journey back to School on **1 May**, when I diverted myself through Bristol once again; S11 404 was my train engine on the 15.15 local to Bath (Queen Square) via Mangotsfield. I also noted:- K10 138 on Bristol Barrow Road Shed; S11 398 on Bath Shed; S11 399 piloting LMS 4F 4560 on an Up empty Special at Midford; T9 304 on Templecombe Shed.

It was my last term at School and I had more important things to do than watch (or travel on) trains throughout the next eight weeks. So I saw nothing of railway interest[26] all through the momentous weeks before and after D-Day. However, on **26 June** I and a friend ignored school regulations and went on an expedition by train to Taunton. We got up early and cycled to **Shillingstone,** where we got the 06.50 ex-Bournemouth West (loco. LMS 2P 4-4-0 700) as far as Templecombe. This connected with a Down Slow to Yeovil Junction (loco. U 1795), whence the push-and-pull (loco M7 129) took us to Yeovil Town, from where we got a GW local to **Taunton.** Taunton was not as busy as we expected – but interesting enough – and we were there for nearly seven hours (partly spent away from the railway, trying to find the Loco Shed). We returned at 17.48 to Yeovil Town and so back to Shillingstone by the outward route. Other SR engines noted were:- T9 304 (on 07.00 OP Bath – Bournemouth), N15 774 'Sir Gaheris', K10 344, L11 163 at Templecombe; N15 789 'Sir Guy' (on 05.56 OP Plymouth – Yeovil Junction) at Milborne Port; L11 134 at Yeovil Junction; S15 826, K10 145, T9 702/12, U 1790/3 at Yeovil Town (mainly on Shed); T9 724 – *remarkably* – at Taunton on the 10.55 GW OP from Exeter St David's. On return, additionally:- L12 412 at Yeovil Town; H15 332, U 1794, T9 710 (on Up Milk), and N15 792 'Sir Hervis de Revel' (our train to Templecombe) at Yeovil Junction; (N15 789 again, on the 17.00 EP Waterloo - Exeter) at Sherborne; T9 715 (on Down Milk empties) and S15 827 at Milborne Port. Finally, *most noteworthy*, at Templecombe there was one (unidentified) *LNE B12/3 4-6-0*[27]. Again the next day, **27 June**, we cycled to Shillingstone and caught the same train as before, but this time went to **Cole,** for a repeat of our day the previous year watching trains where the S&D crossed the GW main line. SR engines I noted were:- T9 304 (on 07.20 OP Templecombe - Bournemouth West) at Shillingstone; S11 398, T1 3, 4 at Templecombe (S&D); N15 454 'Queen Guinevere', 791 'Sir Uwaine', L12 420 (on a Down Special) at Templecombe SR. On return, T1 3 was on an Up Goods at Stalbridge and S11 399 was on the 17.15 OP Bournemouth West to Bath at Sturminster Newton.

On **1 July 1944**, I travelled up to London, to take my University Entrance examinations – in the middle of the Flying Bomb ('Doodlebug') Offensive, a period of three weeks that proved to be most memorable for me. The offensive was at its height and on three occasions while we were sitting our exams at Imperial College (South Kensington) we heard a Doodlebug's engine cut out – which meant it was about to fall and explode, so we got down on the floor under our desks. (One exploded right outside the Natural History Museum). As a consequence of the 'Disturbance by the Flying Bombs', the Pass marks for the exams were officially lowered – and so I got in to the University! But at 17 I was not frightened by the Doodlebugs – far more of the Exams, but rather excited; I enjoyed watching the Doublebugs while I watched trains! Of course everyone else was 'just carrying on as normal'. In fact, although the FBs were very destructive where they fell and a lot of people were killed and injured, damage and disruption to normal life was not great, a lot less than in the Blitz[28].

My train had run to time – in spite of everything. Obervations *(Table 16)* on the journey from **Blandford via Templecombe to Waterloo** were as follows:-

Usually, when I was not sitting exams, my mother encouraged me to get out of Central London to watch trains, and hopefully I would be safer! I noted the following SR engines:-

In about two hours at **Old Oak Common East Junction** in the morning of **4 July** there were 10 workings on the WLR, four being SR:- C 1581 on Up freight (banked), W 1917 on Down freight, W 1923 on Up freight (banked), U1 1901 Up light engine. (The banker that day up North Pole bank was an LMS 2-8-0). Also N 1410 light engine and W 1918 with freight, from the WLR onto the GWR. In 3½ hours that afternoon at **West Hampstead**[29] I recorded six SR engines (out of 20 steam workings) on the North London line:- U 1616/7/8 (light engines, returning with Specials[30]), U1 1901 (again) on a Special, C 1689 light engine, '700' 309 on freight. In 80 minutes at West Hampstead on the morning of **7 July** I noted 44 steam workings, 16 on the NLR of which five were SR:- Q1 C27/31, '700' 697 and C 1018 on freight; U1 1907 on an empty Special. On **8 July**, in two hours at Old Oak Common there were 13 workings on the WLR, six being SR:- U 1803 on an Up Special, U1 1906/10 on empty Specials, D1 1145 went up light engine and returned on a Special, and D1 1492 Up light engine; also, off the WLR onto the GWR, were two freights: the first with Q1 C3 + C3 2309, the second with C3 2302[31]. On **12 July** I was at **Old Oak Common** again, 14.45 – 17.35: on the WLR there were 21 workings, with 10 SR engines:- T9 708 came up light and returned with a Special, C3 2309 on Up empties returned light engine, W 1921 on Down freight, U1 1900 on Up empties, W 1924 on Up freight, C 1298 on Down USA vans[32], T9 307 + U 1617 ran Up light coupled to LMS 0-6-2T 7675 and returned later on a Down Special; meanwhile up from the WLR to the GWR had been Ws 1917 on empties and 1922 on freight. On **13 July** in **Old Oak Common Yard** I noted C 1298. During 90 minutes at **Brent Sidings (Cricklewood)** I saw:- S15 496 on N&SWJ freight and U 1612 ran up light engine and took over a Special onto the SR. Then between 14.50 and 18.00 that day at **Old Oak Common** I saw a fascinating 23 workings on the WLR, which included 12 SR engines as follows:- an unidentified loco on a Down freight, Q1 C16 Down light, C 1018 (*with LNE D16 8875 as pilot!*) on Up freight, U 1636 + U1 1909 on an Up Special, C 1718 (banked by

Location	Class	Number	Working	Notes
TABLE 16: Blandford - Templecombe - Waterloo 1 July 1944				
Blandford, 07.45	LMS 2P 4-4-0	700	06.48 Bournemouth West - Bath	My train
Shillingstone	T9	304	07.20 Templecombe – B'mouth West	
Stalbridge	LMS 4F 0-6-0	4417	Down goods	
Templecombe, c. 08.40 – 09.00	LMS 3F, 4F 0-6-0; 7F 2-8-0	3792, 4146; 13804	On Shed	
	T1	4	S&D Pilot	
	LMS 4F 0-6-0	3924	Down freight, S&D	
	U	1791	06.30 OP from Exeter Central	
	N15	454 'Queen Guinevere'	07.30 EP Exeter Central – Waterloo (to Salisbury)	My train
	S15	827	08.05 OP Salisbury – Ilfracombe etc.	
Gillingham	N15	790'Sir Villiars'	Down Special	Troops?
Tisbury	S15	847	Down freight	
Salisbury, c. 09.45 – 09.50	N15; H15; N; '0395'	741 'Joyous Gard'; 522; 1873; 3441	On Shed	
	WD 2-8-0	7494/5	On Shed	
	N15	738 'King Pellinore'	Down parcels	
	GW 'Castle' 4-6-0	5080 'Defiant'	?Portsmouth - Cardiff EP	
	T9	729	Light engine	
	N15	453 'King Arthur'	Transfer freight	
	GW 2-8-0T	5232	Up freight from Westbury line	
	N15; L12; Z; G6; T1; M7	747 'Elaine'; 421; 957; 279; 10; 243	In yard etc.	
Porton	T9	288	Shunting	
Andover Junction	U; M7	1636; 244	In yard	
	GW: 2-6-0; 2-6-2T	6374, 8358; 4502/10	On Shed	
Worting Junction	Q1	C21	Down mineral	
	T14	461	10.45 OP Basingstoke - Salisbury	
Basingstoke	T3; **WD 2-8-0**	563; 7492	On Shed	The T3 had been *reinstated*
	N; U; G6	1874; 1623/33; 278	In yard and/or shunting	
	GW 2-8-0	2842	On GW Shed	
Winchfield	'700'	355	Down light engine	
	S15	502	Down freight	
Farnborough	T9	707	Down OP 09.54 Waterloo - Basingstoke	
Woking	U1	1903	Down freight to Guildford line	
	H15; L11; M7	478; 442; 676	In yard and/or shunting	
	S15	511	Down freight	
Walton-on-Thames	N15X	2333 'Remembrance'	Shunting	
	'Lord Nelson'	865 'Sir John Hawkins'	?10.54 OP Waterloo - Salisbury	Could have been the 11.00 EP ex-Waterloo – not in timetable
Esher	H15	486	Shunting	
Wimbledon	L11	411	Shunting	
Earlsfield	K10	386	Light engine	
Clapham Junction	'Lord Nelson'	859 'Lord Hood'	11.30 EP Waterloo – Bournemouth West	
Nine Elms	'Lord Nelson'; B4X	855 'Robert Blake'; 2060	Light engines	
	G6	160, 259	Shunting	
Waterloo, 11.50	N15	774 'Sir Gaheris'	07.30 EP from Exeter, from Salisbury	My train
	M7	33, 130	Empty stock	

an LMS 2-8-0) on Up freight, C 1061 on Down USA vans, *I3 2091* on an Up Special!, U1 1900 Down light, W 1921 (banked by two LMS engines, 2-6-4T + 0-6-0T!) on Up freight, C2X 2545 on Up empties, finally U 1636 (again) on a Down Special; meanwhile W 1920 returned light from the GWR and K 2339 worked to the GWR on an Up freight. On **15 July** at **West Hampstead** between 10.40 and 12.20, 15 workings on the NLR (out of 52 on all lines) included seven off the SR:- U1 1909 on a Down Special, **WD 2-8-0** 7493 on Up freight, C 1243 on Up

freight, **WD 2-8-0** 7491 on Down freight, C 1244 on Up freight, C 1018 on Down freight and U 1616 on Up empty Special.

On **18 July** I went back to School – for my last 10 days, by the 14.50 from **Waterloo** to **Templecombe**, thence by S&D on to **Blandford**. My diary records that "I saw little of interest, except for four places where the line had been hit, or very nearly, by F-Bs.[33]" *(Table 17)* I noted the following engines:-

TABLE 17: Waterloo - Templecombe - Blandford 18 July 1944				
Location	Class	Number	Working	Notes
Waterloo	L12	416	?	
	V	929 'Malvern'	11.02 EP ex-Bournemouth West	
	'Merchant Navy'	21C8 'Orient Line'	14.50 EP to Ilfracomb/Torrington (to Salisbury)	My train
Vauxhall	T14	444	Up empty stock	
Nine Elms	H15	487	Light engine	
	G6	273	Shunting	
Queens Road	H	1265	Empty stock	
West London Junction	W	1914	Down mineral	
Clapham Junction	'700'	701	Up goods	
	T14; N; Q1; O2; 0-8-0T	446; 1866; C39; 204; 949 'Hecate'	In yard and/or carriage shunting	
Wimbledon	N15	767 'Sir Valence'	Up empties (!)	
	K10	149	Shunting	
Surbiton	B4X	2073	In yard	
Woking	L12	427	Up parcels	
	K10; A12; M7	141; 630; 246	In yard/shunting	
Pirbright Junction	V	939 'Leatherhead'	14.35 OP Basingstoke – Waterloo	
Farnborough	A12	613	Shunting	

LSW Urie S15 class 4-6-0 No. 509 at Eastleigh Shed, fresh from repair at the Works, 11 July 1946.

		Table 17 continued		
Bramshot Halt	**WD 2-8-0**	7493	Up freight	
Hook	'700'	368	Shunting	
Basingstoke, c. 15.52	V	938 'St Olave's	15.20 OP Salisbury – Waterloo	
	D	1145	Up parcels	
	'Lord Nelson'	863 'Lord Rodney'	10.15 EP Torrington/Ilfracombe - Waterloo	
	U; G6; M7	1625/33; 348; 244	In yard/shunting	
	N15; H15; T14; L12; T3; U; G6	335; 456 'Sir Galahad'; 461; 418; 563; 1629; 265		
	M7	248	Ex-14.00 OP Southampton Terminus - Micheldever	
Overton	L11	407	Shunting	
Whitchurch	L11	405	Up freight	
Andover Junction	GW 2-6-0; 2-6-2T	6325 ; 4590	On GW Shed	
	K10	382	Down goods	
	K10 ; U ; GW 4-4-0	342 ; 1636 ; 3421	In yard	
Grateley	U	1635	Down freight	
	L11 ; T9	157 ; 288	In yard	
Salisbury, c. 16.45	T9 ; U ; '0395' ; Z ; T1 ; M7 ; GW 2-6-2T	729 ; 1630 ; 3441 ; 957 ; 361 ; 243, 675 ; 4585	In yard, shunting etc.	
	S15	839	?17.07 OP to Portsmouth	
	S15	827	16.57 OP to Templecombe	
	GW 'Hall' 4-6-0	6962	Onto 13.55 OP Portsmouth - Cardiff	
	'Merchant Navy'	21C5 'Canadian Pacific'	Onto 14.50 EP ex- Waterloo	My train
	GW 28XX 2-8-0	2841	Up GW freight	
	GW 'Hall'; ROD 2-8-0 ; **USA 2-8-0 ; LMS 2-8-0**	4971 'Stanway Hall', 5971 'Merevale Hall' ; 3031 ; **1682 ; 8429**	On GW Shed	
	N15 ; H15 ; T9 ; N ; Q1	451 'Sir Lamorak', 747 'Elaine', 457 'Sir Bedivere', 790 'Sir Villiars' ; 331 ; 312, 723 ; 1872/4 ; C16	On SR Shed	
Wilton	H15	332	Shunting	
Dinton	T9 ; U	715 ; 1791	Shunting	
Templecombe, c. 17.25 – 18.15	N15	744 'Maid of Astolat'	Up empties (!)	
	S15	828	17.36 OP to Exeter	
	U	1793	Down Special empty stock	
	S11	400	15.30 OP ex-Bournemouth West (S&D)	
	S11	399	16.25 Bath – Bournemouth West (S&D)	My train
	T1; LMS 4F 0-6-0	4; 4558	Shunting (S&D)	
	LMS 7F 2-8-0; 4F 0-6-0	13804/6; 4559	On Shed (S&D)	
Shillingstone	S11	403	17.15 OP Bournemouth West – Bath	
Blandford	LMS 4F 0-6-0	4146	Up empties	

SR Maunsell V class 'Schools' 4-4-0 No. 916 'Whitgift' at Waterloo East with the 13.15 Charing Cross to Ramsgate, 20 April 1948.

23

On **23 July** I was persuaded by a friend to bicycle to **Templecombe** *(Table 18)* to watch trains, although it was a Sunday. We were there 13.20 – 16.30 and saw a remarkable lot.

To start with, at the S&D Shed there were:- T9 304; LMS 7F 2-8-0 13805, 3F 0-6-0 3198, 4F 0-6-0s 3924, 4561; and – most noteworthy – *LNE B12/3 8549.*

Class	Number	Working	Notes
Table 18: Templecomble 23 July 1944			
N15	774 'Sir Gaheris'	Up freight	
N15	791 'Sir Uwaine'	Up EP 09.50 Ilfracombe/10.02 Torrington – Waterloo	
'Merchant Navy'	21C3 'Royal Mail'	Up EP 09.50 Launceston/10.00 Plymouth Friary - Waterloo	TC Plymouth – Portsmouth
'Merchant Navy'	21C5 'Canadian Pacific'	Up EP – ?Relief to above	
'Merchant Navy'	21C8 'Orient Line'	Down EP 11.00 Waterloo – Plymouth Friary	
LMS 3F 0-6-0	3444	S&D Pilot	
N15	792 'Sir Hervis de Revel'	Down EP 11.40 Portsmouth & S. – Plymouth Friary	
N15	738 'King Pellinore'	Up empty Special	
S15	826	Up freight	
T9	722	Down OP 13.40 Salisbury – Plymouth Friary	
T9	312	Up OP 15.25 Yeovil Town – Waterloo	
S15	847	Down freight	
G6	276	Shunting	

On **28 July** I went home, in great glee because it was the Last Time – I was *leaving School!* This time I bicycled the second half of the journey, from Bristol to Tewkesbury[34]. Moreover, I took an unusual route from Stourpaine & Durweston Halt (not Blandford) to Bristol, changing at Radstock onto the GW branch for Temple Meads. The only SR engines I noted were:- at Templecombe (where my train was held up for an hour), T1 5 was S&D pilot, and on the SR Q1 C35 passed on an *Up Special!*, T9 729 on 08.05 OP Salisbury – Exeter etc., T9 712 on an Up School Special, N15 449 'Sir Torre' on 07.30 EP Exeter – Waterloo; at Chilcompton S11 398 was on 10.05 OP Bath – Bournemouth West.

In August 1944, Ashchurch, Cheltenham, Gloucester etc. were just as exciting as in April. There were many interesting and unusual workings – even LNE B12/3s on Hospital trains up the Malvern branch. The D-Day Emergency Timetable was still in force and the main line trains were absolutely crammed, people were left stranded and a few Reliefs just had to be put on. The loaned SR engines, on the other hand, were notable for their absence: this was because by then they had all been sent elsewhere on the Midland if not returned to the SR. On 1 September 1944, I travelled up to Newcastle-on-Tyne, where I had the 'Time of My Life' (as a Train-Watcher) working as a Cleaner for three weeks at the LNER Depot at Heaton – but that's another story[35].

On **26 September 1944** I went down to **London**, where I have stayed for most of my adult life. For the rest of the War and until July 1946, I was an undergraduate at King's College (University of London). This gave me plenty of opportunities to watch trains at my favourite London sites, which as I have explained were not normally on the SR – except for Clapham Junction – and observations of SR locomotives were incidental. Thus at **West Hampstead** again, in the afternoon of Saturday **14 October** during a spell of just 60 minutes there were 36 workings and I noted on the NLR:- Q1 C33 and C 1572 on Up freights; on **1 November** of 55 workings I recorded between 13.40 and 15.40, five on the NLR were SR:- on the Down '700' 687 and C 1068 on freights, '700' 308 on USA vehicles and Q1 C19 light engine, on the Up was **WD 2-8-0** 7486 on a freight. On **4 November** (a Saturday) at **Old Oak Common/Mitre Bridge**, 14.10-16.10:- W 1925 was on Down freight on the WLR, N 1410 came Up light engine, C 1244 on Up freight, C 1581 on Down freight and W 1924 on Up freight: however as well, to/from the GW Yard and the WLR were:- W 1918 and D 1732 + N 1412 on freights, and U1 1904 + C 1681 came Up light engines coupled and took a freight back, then Q 541 took a mineral onto the WLR. On Sunday **5 November** on a run to **Ashtead from Waterloo** I saw:- at Waterloo: N15X 2333 'Remembrance', M7 319; at Vauxhall: M7 33 (on milk); at Nine Elms: 'Lord Nelson' 862 'Lord Collingwood', N15X 2329 'Stephenson'; at Clapham Junction: C 1694; M7 38, 667; O2 212; 0-8-0T 949 'Hecate'; at Wimbledon: D15 466 on empty stock, K10 149 and U 1617 in yard; at Ashtead -- remarkably: E1 1179 + U1 1901 on an Up Special.

On Sunday **12 November,** I 'bunked' **Bricklayers Arms (BA) Shed**, which was hidden away in the -- badly damaged – labyrinth of the BA Goods Depot complex, surrounded by devastated back-streets. In the smoky gloom there were 66 SR locomotives of 19 varieties, together with 15 WD 'Austerity' 2-8-0s. The SR locomotives were:- N15 799 'Sir Ironside'; V 910 'Merchant Taylor's', 911 'Dover', 920' Rugby', 937 'Epsom'; L1 1756/8/83; L 1759/69/87; D 1057; E 1036, 1159/66/75/6, 1275, 1315, 1491, 1547; E1 4-4-0 1163, 1504/6/7/11; N 1817; N1 1878; U1 1898; O1 1093, 1251, 1388/97/8, 1428/9; C 1033/71, 1223/53/70/87/97, 1693, 1723; I1X 2009; E3 2170, 2458/9/60/1/2; E4 2463; S 1685[36]; E1 0-6-0T 2097, 2128/41/51/65; H 1324, 1533/41/2/6/50; D1 0-4-2T 2357. The 'Austerities' were WD Nos. 7422/4/5/8/30/72/3/5-7, which had been on loan to the SR since early 1944 and working from BA; also WD Nos. 7317-9/21/3, which came from Wellingborough (15A) on the LMS: all were destined to go over to the Continent within the next three months for their intended work for the Army of Liberation.

On **17 November**, I went down to my old School for the weekend, travelling from **Waterloo** on the 17.00 slow train as far as **Salisbury**, thence on to Blandford by bus. As it soon got dark, my notebook records few numbers:- H15 524, U 1617, M7 132, 241, 667, H 1544 at Waterloo; LNE N1 4558 at West London Junction; M7 38, LMS 4-4-0 515 (on a *Special*[37]) at Clapham Junction; K10 385, L11 156 at Wimbledon; '700' 699 at Surbiton; S15 509 at Weybridge; '0395' 3436, M7 378, 676 at Woking. On my return journey, by the same route, it was dark all the way and I recorded no numbers at all. On **12 December** at **Kensington (Addison Road)**, in just a few minutes I noted:- Q1 C3 Down light engine and U 1619 on a Down Special.

In **1945** I got out and about a good deal more, especially when the weather (and my College commitments) allowed.

This admittedly relates but obliquely to the SR, but on **9 January** I went to **West Hampstead**, partly to see what the situation was after a Rocket had fallen there on the previous afternoon. My diary records: "I looked round to see where the rocket had fallen on the Met[ropolitan] yesterday afternoon and saw that it was just by, if not on, the bridge carrying the NL over the Met. The NL and Met seemed to be more or less blocked[38] but the GC was all right, and of course the Midland." (I evidently did not get near the damage, as that was all I wrote). I observed from my usual spot near Finchley Road for about an hour in the afternoon and indeed the only engines seen on the NLR were an LMS 2-6-2T and two 0-6-0Ts 'messing about'; there were 14 workings on the Midland and four on the GC – and that was all, no SR.

On Saturday **13 January,** I went down to **Woolwich Arsenal** from **Charing Cross**, noting much bomb-damage but not a lot of engines:- V 905 'Tonbridge', L1 1789, C 1243, H 1500 at Charing Cross; V 923 'Bradfield' at Ewer Street; O1 1388 at North Kent East Junction; C 1227 at Maze Hill; C 1223 at Charlton.

The next time I took notes on the SR was on **22 March,** *(Table 19)* when I went down from **Charing Cross to Chislehurst** and spent 14.10 – 17.00 in the secluded spot between all the junctions that I had discovered the previous year (see above) and returned to **Cannon Street.**

Opposite - One of the outsize SE&C Wainwright J class 0-6-4Ts, No. 1598, at Ashford Shed, 6 July 1946.

TABLE 19: Charing Cross - Chislehurst - Cannon Street 22 March 1945				
Location	Class	Number	Working	Notes
Charing Cross	V	921 'Shrewsbury'	?09.40 ex-Margate via Dover	
Waterloo (East)	V	913 'Christ's Hospital'	Light engine	
London Bridge	H	1324	Light engine	
Hither Green	W; D1	1925; 2239	On Shed	
	N; O1; LMS 2-6-2T; LNE N1	1412; 1258, 1381, 26; 4559/76	In Yard	
Chislehurst / Bickley, 14.10 – 17.00:	(N	1412)	Down freight, SER to LC&D	
	L1	1759	11.32 EP Sandwich – Charing Cross	
	N15	778 'Sir Pelleas'	11.15 EP Ramsgate – Victoria	
	N15	801 'Sir Meliot de Logres'	14.25 EP Victoria – Chatham – Dover	
	V	905 'Tonbridge'	13.20 OP Hastings – Cannon Street	
	R1	1706	Down light engine, LC&D	
	V	904 'Lancing'	14.10 EP Hastings – Charing Cross	
	(V	913 'Christ's Hospital')	15.25 OP Charing Cross – Wadhurst	
	N15	780 'Sir Persant'	13.12 EP Ramsgate – Victoria	
	L1	1786	16.00 EP Charing Cross – Dover – Margate	
	V	936 'Cranleigh'	14.10 EP Hastings – Charing Cross	
	V	922 'Marlborough'	15.35 EP Victoria – Ramsgate	
	V	938 'St Olave's'	16.20 EP Charing Cross – Hastings	
	O1	1386	Down light engine, SER	
	(L1	1759)	16.38 OP Cannon Street - Ashford	
	L1	1785	Down EP, SER	Train uni-identified
Elmstead Woods	(V	921 'Shrewsbury')	Down EP, SER	Train uni-identified
Hither Green	N; Z; LNE N1	1414; 955/6; 4573	In Yard	
	C; W	1244, 1513, 1695; 1913	On Shed	
New Cross	V	909 'St Paul's'	?17.06 Cannon Street – Hastings	
London Bridge	L1	1755	Empty stock	
	V	907 'Dulwich'	?17.18 OP Cannon Street – Hastings	
Cannon Street	V; L1; H	911 'Dover'; 1762; 1326	In yard	
	V	919 'Harrow'	18.18 EP to Hastings	

On **23 May 1945** I saw no SR engines in nearly three hours at **West Hampstead**, in spite of plenty of freight on the NLR. The next time I had anything to do with the SR was after VE-Day: on Sunday **27 May** *(Table 20)* , I went from **Waterloo to Hampton Court** and back, noting:-

TABLE 20: Waterloo - Hampton Court - Waterloo 27 May 1945				
Location	Class	Number	Working	Notes
Waterloo	M7	322	Pilot	
Clapham Junction	R1	1696	Carriage shunting	
Wimbledon	'700'	699	In yard	
Surbiton	H15	483	14.54 OP Waterloo – Southampton	
	H15	491	Up mineral	
Berrylands	M7	249	Light engine	
Clapham Junction	LMS 0-6-0T	7355	Shunting	
Vauxhall	N15X	2332 'Stroudley'	15.24 OP ex-Southampton	
Waterloo	'Merchant Navy'; 'Lord Nelson'; N15X	21C14 'Nederland Line'; 863 'Lord Rodney', 865 'Sir John Hawkins'; 2331 'Beattie'	Up and Down EP/OP	

Above - *Another smart ex-Works engine, SE&C Wainwright O1 class 0-6-0 No. 1437, is being turned at Ashford Shed, 6 July 1946.*

Right – *SR Maunsell Z class 0-8-0T No. 952 alongside the water-tank topped office block by the coaling stage at Eastleigh Shed, 11 July 1946.*

On **6 June**, the WLR traffic at **Mitre Bridge/Old Oak Common** was not as interesting as previously, but two C's (1229 + 1113) came up into the GW Yard on a train of AFVs. Although the Pacific War was still waging, plenty of extra holiday trains were now being provided and advertised – the demand for travel was higher than ever. I had a three-hour stint (13.45 – 16.40) at **Clapham Junction** *(Table 21)* on Tuesday **26 June**.

Time	Class	Number	Working	Notes
13.45	LMS 4F 0-6-0	4043 (Hasland!)	Mineral (?Brent – Feltham)	Returned later on empties
	R	1661	Parcels, WL to WLER	
	N15	737 'King Uther'	Light Engine to WL	Returned later with Milk, to WLER
	U1	1903	Light Engine WL – WLER	
	LNE N1 0-6-2T	4555 (Hornsey)	Vans WL – WLER	
	C	1690	Light Engine WL – WLER	Returned later with empties, then Light Engine
	M7	132	Empty stock to Waterloo	Returned later
	W	1918	Freight WLER – Central Section	
	LMS 7F 0-8-0	9272 (Willesden)	Freight WLER – Central Section	
	H15	331	13.54 Waterloo - Basingstoke	
	H	1548	Down PW train Central Section	Returned later with freight to WLER
	B1	1446	Up Light Engine Central Section	
	M7	254	Light Engine	
	N15	799 'Sir Ironside'	Down Light Engine to WL	Returned later with Special empty stock (Train C32) to WLER
	M7	130	Empty stock from Waterloo, hen Light Engine	Returned Light Engine and worked second trip to Waterloo
	F1	1043	Parcels from WL, the Up Light Engine	
	B4X	2056	Down Light Engine (coupled to 834), then Up empty stock![39]	
	S15	834	Down Light Engine (coupled to 2056), then Up empty stock	Returned later on Down express
14.20	Q1	C37	Up empties from WL, then Light Engine	Returned later Light Engine
	H	1177	Down van to WL	Returned later Light Engine then took Up van
	M7	241	Up empty stock	Returned later Light Engine and took another Up empty stock
	E6X	2407	Down mineral WLER – Central Section	
	N15	777 'Sir Lamiel'	13.07 OP Basingstoke – Waterloo	
	Lord Nelson	851 'Sir Francis Drake'	11.02 Bournemouth West – Waterloo	Later went Down on EP
	O2	179	Light Engine and Carriage-shunting	
	I3	2078	Up Parcels, Central Section	
	'700'	701	Light Engine	
	M7	38	Light Engine and Up empty stock	
	O1	1434	Up empties, Central Section – WLER	
	I3	2084	14.30 Victoria – Tunbridge Wells West	
	K10	142	Light Engine from WL	Returned on Down freight to WL
	R1	1696	Up empty stock	
	LMS 2F 0-6-2T	7710 (Willesden)	Down van, WLER - Central Section	
	LNE N1 0-6-2T	4587 (Hornsey)	Up goods, WL – WLER	
	H	1553	Up milk from WL	Returned later – twice
	O2	212	Carriage shunting	
15.00	'Merchant Navy'	21C13 'Blue Funnel'	08.15 Plymouth (Friary)/08.22 Launceston – Waterloo	
	N15	456 'Sir Galahad'	Down EP, 14.50 Waterloo – Torrington/ Plymouth (Friary)/Launceston (?1st Part)	
	H15	484	Up freight WL – Nine Elms	
	C	1243	Up empties Central Section – WLER	
	H15	488	Down EP, 14.50 Waterloo – Torrington/ Plymouth (Friary)/Launceston (?2nd Part)	
	K10	380	Up freight WL – Nine Elms	
	N15	750 'Morgan le Fay'	Up Evacuees' Special[40](!)	
	LMS 3P 2-6-2T	92 (Kentish Town)	Milk WLER - WL	Returned later
	LMS 8F 2-8-0	8603 (Willesden)	Up empties Central Section – WLER	
	Q1	C3	Up Special empty stock, WL	
	L12	419	Down empty stock (main line)	
	'Austerity' 2-10-0s	WD 73778 + 73777[41]	Up Light Engine WL - WLER	A remarkable sight!
	Lord Nelson	865 'Sir John Hawkins'	15.20 EP Waterloo – Weymouth	
	N15	766 'Sir Geraint'	15.30 EP Waterloo – Bournemouth West	
	U	1623	?15.54 OP Relief Waterloo – Basingstoke	
	B4X	2070	Down empty stock (!)	
	N15	455 'Sir Launcelot'	Up Light Engine WL	
	I3	2025	14.10 Tunbridge Wells West – Victoria	

	N15X	2331 'Beattie'	?12.10 Exeter (Central) – Waterloo	
	H2	2421 'South Foreland'	15.55 Victoria – Oxted – Brighton/Eastbourne	
	V	931 'King's Wimbledon'	Up Special	
	O2	204	Empty stock	
	LNE N1 0-6-2T	4585 (Hornsey)	Down freight WLER – WL	
	E1	1019	Down Light Engine Central Section	Returned later on empty stock
	H	1544	Empty stock	
	U	1614	Up OP, 14.35 Basingstoke – Waterloo	
	M7	123	Empty stock	
	O1	1109	Down Light Engine to WL	
	'Merchant Navy'	21C19 'French Line, C.G.T.'	?11.30 Weymouth – Waterloo	
16.40	Lord Nelson	853 'Sir Richard Grenville'	?11.48 Bournemouth West – Waterloo	

It shows a remarkable variety: about 30 different SR classes, plus five LMS, one LNE -- and those WDs!

On **3 July 1945**, I had the opportunity to visit the **Waterloo Signalbox** – 'state-of-the-art' at the time. As an impressionable youth I was thrilled by being allowed – under supervision -- to set the road for several movements including the arrival of the Atlantic Coast Express. The locomotives I noted on that occasion were:- 'Merchant Navy' 21C10 'Blue Star', 'Lord Nelson' 853 'Sir Richard Grenville', 858 'Lord Duncan', H15 523, T14 462, M7 123 and H 1551.

On **4 July**, at **West Hampstead** (14.40 - 17.40) I noted 77 workings, but only two SR: Q1 C8 and U 1637, both on NLR freights.

On Saturday **7 July** I travelled down to my old School for another brief visit. This time I took a novel route to Blandford, travelling down from **Paddington**[42] to **Bruton** (changing at Westbury), whence I walked to **Cole** and took an S&D train to **Blandford**! I returned the same way, but from

Bruton via Westbury and Swindon instead of direct. On the way down I noted:- L12 426/34, D 1729, N 1849 at Reading (SR) and N15 457 'Sir Bedivere' at Templecombe. On the journey back on **10 July**, I had to wait 75 minutes at Templecombe and saw 'Merchant Navy' 21C6 'Peninsular & Oriental S.N. Co.' on a Down EP and 21C5 'Canadian Pacific' on an Up EP, H15 332/3 and U 1793 on OPs. Then at Reading (SR) I noted:- N 1815/57/61, U 1627, 1809, F1 1042/60/2, 1156.

On **11 July** I was at **Old Oak Common** 14.40 – 19.00 and noted 32 workings on the WLR (*cf.* 117 on the GWR), of which the only SR were:- C 1575 (assisted by LMS 4-6-0 5327), W 1909/25 were on Up freights, also W 1911 working into the GW Yard, U1 1907/10 ran Up light engines (separately). On **19 July** between 14.55 and 18.05 at **West Hampstead** I noted 105 workings in all, only 14 being on the NLR -- on which a more normal service of electric trains was now running, but only one SR:- Q1 C29 on a Down freight

Soon to be scrapped Maunsell-rebuilt LB&SC Marsh I1X class 4-4-2T No. 2597 at Brighton Shed, 23 March 1946.

WATCHING TRAINS on the SR – PART I

FOOTNOTES

Abbreviations:- ACE – Atlantic Coast Express; AFV – Armoured Fighting Vehicles; DN&S – Didcot, Newbury & Southampton; EP – Express passenger; K&ESR – Kent & East Sussex Railway; Lord Nelson; M&SWJ – Midland & South-Western Junction; MWL – Metropolitan Widened Lines; N&SWJ – NLR - North London Lines, North & South Western Junction; OP – Ordinary passenger; RCTS – Railway Correspondence & Travel Society; S&D – Somerset & Dorset; WL – Windsor Lines; WLR – West London Line; WLER – West London Extension Line.

[19] Also at Worcester and Gloucester for most of the War were a number of LNER (ex-NER) J25 0-6-0s.

[20] I do not know why I saw T1 0-4-4Ts at Stalbridge more than once, as I am not aware of a Government Depot being there.

[21] In the 5¾ miles between Saltley and Water Orton I noted no less than *53 engines* – nearly all in traffic!

[22] On loan to the LMS!

[23] Specials would have been distinguished by a Military reporting number, e.g. '6.E.x' – the x-th special train for Eastern Command on the 6th of the month.

[24] I suppose this was being sent round from Nine Elms – or wherever – via Clapham Junction and Kingston to Feltham, but if so it would have had to reverse at Twickenham!

[25] I also noted *six* LNER (GE Section) workings – Troop Specials or light engines.

[26] I faintly recollect seeing a U 2-6-0 one day in the distance on the S&D at Blandford.

[27] There were 11 Hospital trains made up for US Army casualties after D-Day. These worked widely across the country as dedicated units with staff and crews who lived with them. B12/3s were chosen as motive-power for their light axle-load and wide route-availability, being fitted with dual vacuum/Westinghouse brakes. In fact one of the trains was allocated to Templecombe.

[28] For details see my account, '*Damage and Disruption on the Railways of Great Britain during World War Two*', the text of which is available on the Collections on Line of the Imperial War Museum website.

[29] Most notable here at this time were the Evacuee Specials from St Pancras and Marylebone.

[30] Presumably taken over at Willesden Junction.

[31] All the eight C3 0-6-0s were shedded at Horsham at that time.

[32] Probably from Hainault, where they were being assembled.

[33] These had included one right on the tracks between Earlsfield and Wimbledon on 4 July, Nine Elms Goods on 9 July, Wimbledon Station also Raynes Park – New Malden on 16 July.

[34] 'It was a fine run, at an average of 12 mph with two 15 minute-stops, 'the six-mile climb from Temple Meads to Patchway being achieved in 45 minutes start-to-stop – in spite of signal-stops'.

[35] As is well known, a batch of 'King Arthurs' had been on loan there in 1942-3, but had long gone back home and Heaton had instead a lot of 'Yanks' and LMS-type 8Fs, followed by WD 'Austerity' 2-8-0s.

[36] A saddle-tank curiosity.

[37] Particularly remarkable as a locomotive type and its allocation (Walsall).

[38] The facts were:- On **8/1/45** at 16.35, a Rocket exploded right on the LMS (NLR) lines 200 yards west of **West End Lane** Station, badly damaging the bridge over the LPTB and LNER lines; also a substation was damaged and supply for traction and signalling interrupted. A Bakerloo Line train was blasted, injuring 11 passengers and the guard. NLR electric services were terminated at Brondesbury and Hampstead Heath, or suspended; some freight was diverted *via* Chalk Farm, but much of the vital cross-London freight traffic on the NLR had to use alternative routes. The Metropolitan and Bakerloo Line trains terminated at Kilburn and Willesden Green. Also suburban passenger services on the LNER from Marylebone were suspended, except that an LNER shuttle was run Marylebone – Harrow-on-the-Hill to clear LPTB passengers. Buses were then substituted until all the lines were reopened, in stages up to 11.15 9/1/45.

[39] It was unusual for B4X to be employed on Waterloo empty stock

[40] Evacuee children being returned home after the End of the War in Europe.

[41] No doubt returning from storage at WD Longmoor and on their way to the LNER at March, never having been to the Continent.

[42] The Holiday crowds at Paddington were so vast that they were marshalled into a long queue along Eastbourne Terrace.

A FURTHER INSTALMENT IN THIS FASCINATING SERIES OF OBSERVATIONS BY BEN BROOKSBANK WILL APPEAR IN A REGULAR ISSUE OF 'SOUTHERN WAY' SHORTLY.

NEW WORKS ON THE SOUTHERN

Amongst the new works completed on and for the Southern Railway during WW2, were four sidings on the west side of the main line just south of Eastleigh. Known as Stoneham Sidings, their purpose was two-fold. Firstly to afford additional siding accommodation for locomotives awaiting access to nearby Eastleigh depot, and secondly as a refuge for locomotives from the depot should the latter be damaged by the enemy. As it was Eastleigh depot was hit by two bombs, both fortunately resulting in just a crater. Both these craters - by then grassy deep depressions, were still visible in the 1960s.

The sidings at Stoneham were brought into use on 21 March 1943, accessed from the south by means of the up line only and controlled from the existing Stoneham signal box which also oversaw a nearby level crossing. At the north end was a single storey brick ground frame built in ARP style. The sidings and GF were taken out of use from 9 December 1951 but remained in situ. They achieved a second use as a pre-assembly depot in connection with the electrification of the Bournemouth line from May 1965 to October 1966, during which time a mobile welding unit from London Transport was operating from the site. In the left background are the houses of Southampton Road.

Do it Now!

BRITISH RAILWAYS

Doesn't ANYBODY know?

BRITISH RAILWAYS

This was YOUR Train

BRITISH RAILWAYS

PRIORITY

BRITISH RAILWAYS

This page: Dover, 4 June 1940. The view left has been seen before in Bernard Darwin's 'War on the Line'. It depicts some of the French survivors from Dunkirk at Dover Marine, whilst below, French troops are seen awaiting transport. The 4 June 1940 saw some 15,172 allied personnel leave by train from Dover, this compared with just two British soldiers. On the same day allied forces had also arrived at Folkestone: 4,160, Ramsgate: 3,700, Margate: 2,673, Sheerness: 470, and Clacton: 27. Just five other British serviceman had arrived at Ramsgate. None were reported as injured. (Between 27 May and 4 June inclusive, some 189,859 British forces personnel arrived together with 8,061 wounded. Including other allied forces, the total was 308,491.)

DOVER AND HEADCORN

JUNE 1940

Feeding the 5,000 - well actually some of the nearly 26,000 that arrived from Dunkirk at either Dover, Ramsgate or Margate on 2 June. (A further 1,756 men had been landed at Sheerness, Newhaven and Harwich.)

In this scene at Headcorn on 2 June 1940, volunteers as well as service personnel are seen preparing and serving food. The stock top left is clearly LNER in origin, probably indicating the trains' destination as being north of the Thames.

Headcorn was one of three 'feeding stations' established along the routes taken by the dispersal trains emanating from East Kent - the others being at Paddock Wood and Faversham. The 2 June had 26 special trains leave Dover, eight from Ramsgate, and six from Margate. (For trains commencing their journey with men landed at Sussex ports, the feeding stations were at Horley or Chichester.) In total Headcorn provided refreshments for 207 out of the 351 evacuations trains that passed through. This was achieved by 40 soldiers from the Royal Army Service Corps assisted by 50 volunteers who worked 8hr shifts around the clock. Nineteen stoves were set up on the up platform. Daily, 2,500 loaves were sliced and made into sandwiches.

According to Peter Tatlow in 'RETURN FROM DUNKIRK - Railways to the Rescue: Operation Dynamo 1940' - Oakwood Press, 2010, "At night the Good Samaritans at Headcorn would thump on the outside of the steamed-up carriage windows to awaken the tired occupants with trays of steaming hot cups and mugs of tea. On being advised of the location, a few men with local connections were able to ask for their families to be informed by telephone of their safe return in one piece. In recognition of her services in organising the refreshments at Headcorn, Mrs Joan Kempthorne was awarded the British Empire Medal."

Above - *The result of an enemy Dornier which crashed on to the forecourt at Victoria (Eastern) at 1300 on 15 September 1940. The incident created a fire as seen her, but it was reported this had been extinguished by 1330. Shops and a restaurant were damaged but there were no casualties. (Seen is the main section of a Dornier Do17Z, one of three aircraft flying in formation towards Buckingham Palace. The three had been attacked by fighters from the RAF 504 Squadron based at Hendon. One of these allied aircraft was a Hurricane flown by Flt Sgt Ray Holmes, who after attacking the first two, rammed - possibly accidentally - the third, causing the rudder and rear section of the enemy plane to shear off. It immediately went out of control and crashed as seen. Most of the crew had bailed out before impact - although one was beaten up by angry crowds in Kensington. He died of his injuries in hospital the following day. Flt Sgt Holmes was also forced to bail out at a height of only 350 feet, he landed safely on the slanting roof of a house in Hugh Street, sliding down the gutter and finished dangling a few feet above a dustbin. He was uninjured and was reported as treated as a hero by the local populace. After 'restoring his spirits' in a local public house, he was transported back to Chelsea Barracks and from there by taxi to his base at Hendon. His own aircraft had crashed on Buckingham Palace Road. The remains of the Hurricane were subsequently excavated in 2004 and placed on display.) This Dornier was the first enemy aircraft to be shot down over London.*

Opposite bottom - *Angerstein Wharf on the south bank of the Thames and accessed by a one mile dead end line off the SECR near Charlton. This was the scene on 26 September 1940 following a raid of exactly one week earlier. With a considerable amount of industry and warehousing on the site, including oil and timber storage, it was an understandable enemy target and was attacked on several occasions. Apart from that referred to above, other dates with reported incidents at the wharf were, 8 September 1940: Delayed Action Bomb exploded, 15 September, 21 September 21 September: UXB, 6 October: UXB, 18 October: Delayed Action Bomb, 20 October, 12 November when 'O1' No. 1051 was damaged, 19 March 1941, 1 July 1944, and finally on 9 March 1945. On the last occasion access to the branch was temporarily curtailed due to enemy damage to the junction with the main line. (Reference is made in the table on page 51 to a coach being used at office accommodation here from May 1941 onwards.)*

Above - *Thornton Heath after the 2115 raid of 4 October 1940.*
The main lines between here and Selhurst were damaged by high
explosive. The Down Main was cleared and operational by 0900
on 6 October and the Up Main at 1445 the same day. The
shadow of the photographer will be noted.

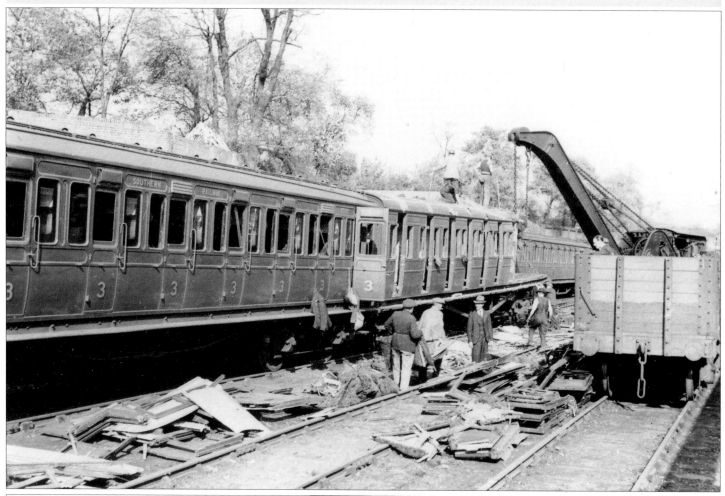

According to the notes accompanying these images they refer to 'West Croydon; 9 October 1940'. The location is of course correct although the date is probably slightly out, referring instead to the enemy attack that occurred at 2200 on Thursday 10 October with the images probably taken the next day. (No enemy incidents are reported as having affected the station on 9 October.) Assuming the revised date to be correct, two high-explosive devices exploded, one each on the Down and Up platforms and blocking both lines. The 2130 EMU service from Epsom Downs to Forest Hill was hit; the train motorman, a soldier and a girl suffered serious injuries. A total of nine persons were injured, six of whom were railway staff. In consequence the station was closed although the London bound platform and bay reopened at 1015 on 11 October. The Down line was clear at 1715, and the up line at 0600 on 12 October. Although reference is made to damage to an EMU set at this location and date in the official records of damaged stock, see page 27 of 'Wartime Southern Part 2', as with the incident in Knights Hill Tunnel on page 6, no record of the affected unit number(s) are given.

1940 - DIFFICULT DAYS

Left - *Some of the destruction wrought and **below**, carrying on as before, the debris cleared but with the skeletal remains of the canopy a visual reminder.*

The evening of 8 November 1940 saw the Southern lines at North Kent East Junction (this page) and Loughborough Junction (opposite and overleaf) attacked.

At North Kent East Junction high explosive damaged three arches of the viaduct, blocking No.1 Up and No.2 Down lines whilst the electric high tension cable was also cut. Signalling and points in the area were disabled until 0100 the following day. In consequence of the severing of the HT cable, the traction current to the third rail was off until 2120, the Herne Hill to Beckenham Junction section re-energised at 2150. The damage was repaired to allow the Down line to be restored at 1530 on 10 December although the Up line was not working again until 24 January 1941. Between September 1940 and March 1945 no less 17 enemy incidents occurred either at or affecting the railway in the vicinity of this junction.

Below - The damaged viaduct and severed HT cable, the latter visible in the 'four-foot'.

This page and overleaf - *Loughborough Junction station after being attacked at 1923 on 8 November 1940. (See also illustration on page 112 of 'Wartime Southern Part 1'.) Lt. Col Mount subsequently reported on the damage as follows, "500 kilo bomb demolished half of the viaduct for three spans on the Holborn - Herne Hill route. Both lines and the platform between blocked, the arches completely shattered - obviously another of several deliberate attacks. The cost of restoration will be up to £15,000. The damage is just short of the Junction, the other lines remaining open and the nearby sub-station was not hit. (This last comment slightly contradicts another report which refers to the sub-station having been damaged.) By 5 February 1941 (just 12 and a bit weeks later) the three shattered arches under the Down line had been restored by timber shoring so allowing trains to pass as 5 mph. This was four weeks earlier than the original estimate. The damaged arches were subsequently reconstructed in concrete, the temporary repair being RSJs carried on concrete buttresses with a central pier of military steel trestling." The permanent rebuild involved concrete piers supporting pre-stressed concrete flat-top spans.*

Loughborough Junction, 8 November 1940. The unsupported down line is seen. As with North Kent East Junction, this was another location to suffer considerably from enemy action throughout the war.

ONE MANS WAR

Fratton Station Foreman Mr B F Powell was presented with an inscribed watch by the SR Traffic Manager for his bravery in rescuing a young soldier from the track in 1941.

The unfortunate bombing of Sunbury station with high explosive at 2220 on 29 November 1940, resulted in the destruction of all the Up side buildings. Both lines were also blocked, the duty signalman and a porter injured. A few weeks earlier on 8 October, services through the station had been disrupted in consequence of a UXB (there is some confusion as to whether this was a unexploded bomb: UXB, or delayed action bomb - DAB, which had fallen on 1 October and was subsequently detonated on 8 October having been made safe two days earlier. Three years later on at 0810 on 23 August 1944, there is a report of the lines between Hampton and Sunbury being blocked. No reason is given. Services were restored on the Down at 1515 and on the Up at 1600. Finally at 1310 on 29 August 1944, the blast from a flying bomb(V1) which had impacted nearby, smashed windows at the station and signalbox as well as damaging the ceilings of the station house.

According to the official report, these two images purport to show the skew bridge at Hooley Cane Tunnel* on or around 29 November 1940. Clearly however, the photographer must have become slightly confused. Yes there did exist a location and tunnel of that name - the point of crossing south east of Redhill where the Tonbridge route met the southern end of the Quarry line. Until BR days there was also a tunnel provided at the location: so the inmates of a nearby 'lunatic asylum' would not be disturbed further by the passage of trains. However, it was only the Quarry line which was electrified and not both routes, so consequently this image has to be further north on the Quarry line and we instead move to south of Coulsdon, near to Star Lane and Merstham: where the Quarry line passes underneath the original Brighton route. The location is referred to as Star Bridge - after the 'Star Inn' on the nearby London to Brighton main road. There are no details of incident and rather than bomb blast, this was possibly aircraft gun or cannon fire, with at least one of the cross girders and adjoining brickwork affected. The top view is looking north towards Coulsdon - the lineman on the telegraph pole will be noted.

* The name Cane Hill covered way is better known.

A second view of the landmine which fell by parachute at London Bridge sometime on the night of 9 December 1940 - see also 'Part 2' in this series: page 31. The view is similar to that seen here, the bomb - a landmine, fortunately failed to explode and ended up part buried, but with the fuse accessible, at the base of the signal box. Notice the extra masonry protection provided around the door of the structure, although it would have been of little consequence had the device exploded.. The men are not identified, although the lack of uniform implies perhaps 'Home-Guard'. (The original name of 'Local Defence Volunteers' had been superseded from 22 July 1940.) No doubt it was necessary to ensure that perhaps an enemy agent did not attempt to reactivate the device with a replacement fuse, hence the presence of the armed men, but the situation otherwise of guarding an enemy bomb might otherwise appear somewhat farcical. (Conventional bombs were dealt with by the military but landmines, which were in effect a sea-mine with a tail-fin added, were dealt with by the navy, who of course already had experience of the fuses in sea-mines.)

This and opposite page - *Having referred to the damage at the other main Southern termini in the earlier issues, we now turn our attention to London Bridge. Seen on these two pages are the results of the devastating fire of 29 December 1940. According to official reports at 1900 on that day, "All Central Section (also eastern LL) lines blocked. Station premises and General Offices (Central Section) badly damaged by fire - these premises had housed some 300 staff of the Traffic Manager's department, who had to be transferred to Waterloo and elsewhere, also much valuable documentation was consumed in the fire - which engulfed several trains. Station closed and staff evacuated. Flames spread to Eastern Section and LL station still on fire at 0600 on 30 December, but trains still run through HL. Lifts to underground destroyed by fire. Platforms 8 - 13 clear at 1530, 1/1/41. Nos. 14 and 15 at 1600 on 2/1/41. No. 17 not clear until 14/1/41.". Lt. Col Mount later reported the damage to the station concourse and buildings would cost around £500,000 to repair. Fortunately the platforms and signalling were not affected and the roof over the platforms was practically intact. Ironically the fire was not caused by several incendiary bombs which fell on the station, and which were quickly dealt with by railway staff, but was due to fires which had been started by similar bombs in nearby St Thomas Street and at Guy's Hospital; and was subsequently hampered due to a*

failure of water pressure. A concrete roof was soon erected over the concourse to provide some accommodation for returning staff. This incident was also to become an object lesson throughout the country, for as a result compulsory fire watching duties were introduced as well as fire-fighting trains. Despite being affected directly or indirectly on a considerable number of occasions from 9 September 1940 through to 5 November 1944, these two pages and the two that follow show the only images so far located of the station. Some of these incidents were of considerable magnitude, as seen here: also on the night of 10/11 May 1941 when several bombs fell causing further damage to the station buildings, platforms and several trains. Further disruption was caused by a UXB from the same raid. Others occasions were less disruptive, such as at 0350 on 6 August 1944 when the windows of the signalbox and two empty EMUs were smashed. No cause was given.

Above *- Literally the dark days of 1941. London Bridge after the attack of 17 February 1941, the photographer perhaps deliberately having produced an image in keeping with the terrible events of that Saturday evening. (Also the two images, opposite top.) At 2225 high explosive fell on the central section concourse near the entrance to platforms 20 and 21. Either this same or another device - it matters not, fell through to the Stainer Street public shelter below, killing 60 people and injuring a further 70 - 50 of these seriously. The nearby railway staff shelter was also affected where five railwaymen were seriously injured, one of these, a ticket collector, later succumbed to his injuries. One EMU unit was reported as damaged by debris. Platforms 15,16, 20 and 21 were out of use until 1530 on 18 February, the first two closed due to debris. To compound matters, a further device fell at 0412 the next day, but did not explode. This was later made safe. In recent years a 'Blue Plaque' has been erected nearby but with differing casualties figures to that stated in the contemporary reports. Disappointingly an incorrect year for the disaster is also shown on the plaque.*

Opposite bottom *- A Maunsell Third perched precariously off the end of the siding at the former Waterloo Necropolis station after the raid of 16 April 1941. (See also pages 56-58 of Part 1.) Corbis Images NA008902.*

'Soldiers on leave arriving at a London Termini - clearly Victoria. 16 April 1941. Leave trains were a feature of WW2, albeit an often forgotten feature. Darwin refers to one at Dover circa 1940 when men who had arrived from France complete with souvenirs, boarded a train of Pullman cars destined for the north of England. Details of such workings are understandably sketchy, whilst any such workings in the period up to 1944 were probably also limited. After that date, however, Darwin records some 1,881 leave trains had been run from the channel ports, several avoiding London completely whilst others would take the men as far as the capital after which they would make their own way by ordinary service. Hence the issue at that time of thousands of card tickets suitably endorsed 'Forces on Leave'. According to Alastair Wilson, it is possible some of the men are from the London Scottish Regiment who were stationed around Ashford in April 1941.

Corbis Images HU030200

EXAMPLES OF SR COACHING STOCK USED FOR WD PURPOSES

CONVERSION / NEW USE DATE	VEHICLE No.	ORIGINAL BUILD DATE	NEW LOCATION	USE	
12/7/39	7261	1900	Ramsgate	Home Guard	
	7271	1900	Dover Marine	Home Guard	Replaced with unknown vehicle after 1/12/40
	7285	1899	Brockenhurst	Home Guard	
5 6 40	7768	1905	Haywards Heath	Home Guard	
	7627	1908	Ashford Loco Dept.	Home Guard	
	7634	1907	Catford Bridge	Home Guard	
23 11 40	7620	1906	Three Bridges	Home Guard	
13 11 40	7619	1906	Feltham	Home Guard	
	7628	1906	Crystal Palace	Home Guard	
	7635	1907	Feltham	Home Guard	
	7637	1907	Reading	Home Guard	
1 12 40	7638	19-7	Ashord	Female Rest Room	
	7639	1907	Gillingham (Kent)	Home Guard	
	7640	1907	Ashford (Kent)	Home Guard	
	7643	1907	Ashford	Sold for ARP	No details given
	7770	1906	Wembley	Sold for ARP	No details given
14 5 41	7741	1905	Angerstein Wharf	Office Accommodation	See page 36.
24 9 41	7338	1904	Ashford	Firewatchers	
	7340	1904	Ashford	Firewatchers	
12 11 41	7327	1904	Sheerness	Firewatchers	
18 2 42	7297	1900	Gomsall	Home Guard	
	7288	1899	Woking	Home Guard	
3 6 42	7289	1900	Rotherhithe Road	Firewatchers	
25 11 42	7276	1900	Deal	Home Guard	
10 2 43	7336	1904	Norwood Junction	Anti-gas train	2 vehicles involved. Other details not known.
10 2 43	7923	1905	Redhill	Home Guard	
31 3 43	7927	1905	Brighton Works	Firewatchers	Specifically mentioned as 'on wheels
16 6 43	7279	1900	Littlehampton	Home Guard	
16 9 44	7286	1899	Folkestone		Interior stripped.
16 9 44	7352	1907	Gomsall	Rifle Range?	Interior stripped - see page 22 Part 1.

Details of vehicles converted for war time use are confused. Those that are confirmed are given above: but there were numerous others listed against specific locations without a purpose being shown. Vehicles sold to the 'WD' and in some cases specifically mentioned as sold to the 'American Army' at Netley (near Southampton) for Ambulance train purposes are deliberately excluded. It is not clear if all, or just some of these above remained complete with their underframe. (With grateful thanks to Dick Coombes and John Atkinson.)

At 2215 on 19 April 1941 the Southern Railway line over Southwark Street Bridge (No. 407) was struck by the enemy. This bridge carried four running lines and two sidings on each side. The bridge was struck by an HE device and six lines collapsed into the street below, along with four wagons and a sludge tender. The remaining two sidings were damaged. In consequence Holborn and Blackfriars stations were closed. The down local line was reopened for steam trains only on 1 June. Down and Up Through lines not cleared until 1530 on 2 June. West side sidings were soon made available for freight by means of single line working as far as Loughborough Junction, the Up Local line over the bridge not restored until 1300 on 29 June, current was also restored to the local lines from 1630 the same day. Lt. Col Mount subsequently reported on the incident in even greater detail, " This is the most comprehensive collapse of a girder bridge I have yet seen. Two of the three girders each with a span of 90' and carrying the four running lines collapsed into the roadway. A third girder carrying some sidings on the east side was pushed off its abutments on the east side. Also, considerable damage was done to one of two main girders of the separate bridge carrying the two 'Market Sidings' on the west side. The latter bridge was restored first, with trestling, and leaving space for the double tram track. The siding lines were slewed into the running lines to provide for a single line for freight traffic. Meanwhile, trestling and steel joist weight-beams to restore the Up and then Down Main lines and the Local lines to be tackled." On 26 May Lt. Col Mount reported that three tracks were now in operation, over steel trestling kindly lent by the War Office. The necessary trestling required for the fourth track would be recovered from Blackfriars Road Bridge - also damaged in the raids. Rebuilding of Southwark Street Bridge was urgent, but required some 1,000 tons of steel: neither War Office, nor as before the LMSR, can provide any more trestling at present so the CME of the SR was being prevailed upon. The Blackfriars main power signal box close by, which had already suffered fire damage on 16 April and was under repair, was completely destroyed. Four men, occupied in hand-signalling, were sheltering in a steel bell-type refuge but were killed by the blast. A spare 24-lever power frame was installed temporarily to work the junctions either side of the bridge. Bridge 98, between Blackfriars Junction and Elephant & Castle was repaired by 1100 on 25 April, but owing to other damage, no traffic could yet pass. Moreover the local lines at McLeod Street Bridge (Elephant & Castle - Walworth Road) were further affected at 1430 on 24 April when the arch collapsed from damage received on 16-17 April. Lines reopened 1045, 26 April. Thus goods traffic was restored in 15 days and other traffic in stages of 22, 42 and 70 days. "It appears that the enemy has made several attempts to put the Metropolitan Widened Lines at Blackfriars out of use, and with other recent incidents at the river bridges it may indicate a deliberate attack on cross-Thames communications." (Further views of this incident appear in 'LONDON MAIN LINE WAR DAMAGE.'

On the night of 10/11 May 1941 London suffered what would turn out to be its last raid of the 1940/41 blitz. Between 2330 and 0415, 507 enemy bombers dropped 711 tons of high-explosive and 86,200 incendiary bombs. The results were 10 major and 46 serious fires, 1,436 were killed and 1,792 injured. The following day the results of just one incident were recorded. This is the main line south of Blackfriars, between Elephant & Castle and Loughborough Junction where HE had fallen damaging a number of the arches supporting the railway. Fortunately it was possible to slew the local lines across so that services were able to resume albeit in a restricted fashion. Much damage was also caused to the surrounding area. The location seen is near Borough Road and King James Street.

As an example of the damage inflicted on the London area of the Southern in just that raid, the official report indicates damage at (or between): Feltham Junction, Feltham Marshalling Yard, Twickenham, Loco Junction, Waterloo, Vauxhall, Nine Elms Loco, Nine Elms Goods, the Waterloo & City line, Tulse Hill, Clapham Junction, Selhurst - Gloucester Road Junction, West Norwood - Gipsy Hill, Peckham Rye - Nunhead / Queens Road, Old Kent Road Junction - Queens Road (Peckham), London Bridge - New Cross Gate / New Cross, New Cross Gate - Surrey Docks, Battersea Park, Victoria - Battersea Park, Denmark Hill, Clapham Junction - Wandsworth Common, Wimbledon - Merton Park, Purley - Kenley, Norwood Yard, Selhurst - Gloucester Road Junction, Holborn Viaduct (see next page), Blackfriars - Elephant & Castle, Longhedge, Shortlands - Beckenham Junction, Loughborough Junction, London Bridge - Spa Road, Deptford Lift Bridge - New Cross Gate Yard, Metropolitan Junction - Cannon Street, London Bridge - Charing Cross, Catford Bridge - Lower Sydenham, Bricklayers Arms, West Wickham, Borough Market Junction, Plumstead Polytechnic Sidings, Greenwich - Maze Hill, and finally Waterloo Eastern - Charing Cross.

This pages and opposite top - The raid of 10/11 May saw the station at Holborn Viaduct hit and set on fire at 2300. In consequence the station offices were gutted and as can be seen, the roof was damaged. The bridge decking, timbers and buildings at Holborn Low Level were also burnt out and debris littered the running lines. There was concern that various underbridges might be affected, whilst all the running lines were either physically affected by rubble or were 'stopped' by control until an inspection could take place. At 0300 the staff were also evacuated. The station was still burning at 1900 the next day although the first indication of a resumption came with the restoration of the Up local line to Snow Hill at 1245 on 14 May. The images were taken two days after the bombing, the concourse littered with debris. In theory at least, the station had already reopened, although for the present it would be a station without trains, caused by further disruption down the line. In due course repairs were effected to the concourse area but the station would continue to bear the scars of its several enemy attacks until rebuilt by British Railways in 1963.

Right - *Also damaged in the same raid was the station at nearby Snow Hill, the entrance to which is seen.*

Above - Holborn Viaduct 11 May 1941 and the street façade of the six-storey former London, Chatham & Dover Railway Hotel, for the present at least seemingly almost intact. The station was destined to be attacked again by a flying-bomb at 0330 on 18 June 1944, causing damage to windows and doors of the station building, considerable (unspecified) other damage but including to a sub-station. On 8 March 1945 the blast from a V2 rocket at nearby Smithfield damaged the windows of the Low Level signal box as well as the station itself.

Right - Two days after the raid of 10/11 May 1941 and debris still litter the track. It was not just damage to the railway that caused disruption to services, damage to adjoining property could have a similar effect. The scene is towards Blackfriars with the closed Ludgate Hill station in the distance - Ludgate Hill had ceased to be a station in 1929 and yet ironically survived the bombings. The large tower adjacent to the railway had once support its roof.

The railway viaduct over the River Adur at Shoreham (Shoreham-by-Sea to perhaps be more strictly accurate.) This imposing structure dated from 1911 and had replaced a timber bridge at the same location. According to the reference in the photographic file, the images seen date from 25 May 1941 and relate to enemy action of 9 May. No other information is given and there is scant reference to the raid in the archives. (Ben Brooksbank's notes on the accompanying CDROM refer to the line being back in action in three weeks from the date of the raid - three days after the views were taken.) From a variety of sources it is believed a stray bomb may have passed directly through the bridge decking resulting in the damage seen, which included to one of the supporting columns.

FOREST HILL

Subsequent to 1941, the years 1942/43 witnessed a welcome respite in the ariel offensive. That is not to say the country, or more directly the Southern Railway was 'attack-free', but as an example, after May 1941 there was only one incident on SR territory in Greater London for the remainder of the year: this was on 28 July 1941 at Feltham, when the Up Hump Box and eight sidings were damaged with two staff injured. The line was also out of action due to damage between Feltham Junction and Feltham East. In 1942 it was a similar story, just one incident, at 0333 on 28 July when shrapnel severed telephone communication between Erith and Crabtree Crossing. Repairs were in place by 0840. The year 1943 was worse, but again not to the standard of 1940/41. Damage at various SR locations in the London area reported in January: Blackfriars - Elephant & Castle, Peckham Rye, Tulse Hill, New Cross Gate, Charlton, Isleworth - Syon Lane, Kidbrooke - Eltham Wells Halt, North Kent East Junction SB, Norwood, New Eltham - Sidcup, and Kidbrook – Eltham Wells

Halt (again). There was nothing in February, but March had: Old Kent Road Junction - Queens Road, Honor Oak Park, Old Kew Junction, North Kent East Junction, Upper Sydenham, Parks Bridge Junction, and Hither Green disrupted. Again nothing in April, then in May it was the turn of: New Cross, Crofton Park, Waterloo, and the line between Saunderstead and Upper Warlingham. The summer months were again quiet with just one incident at Nine Elms. In October was the turn of: Bromley South, Forest Hill, Hinchley Wood - Claygate, Bricklayers Arms - New Cross Gate, Herne Hill Sorting Sidings, Sidcup - New Eltham, and finally at Lee. Two reports in November: Raynes Park - Malden, and at Addiscombe. Finally in December: Kingston - Teddington, and Chelsfield - Knockholt were affected.

Pages 59-61 illustrate the result of a Flying Bomb (V1) hit on the Up side booking-office at Forest Hill at 2245 on Friday 23 June 1944. The bomb started a fire at the station as well as causing extensive damage to the main line and station subway. Four passengers were killed and four persons injured, including one railwayman. The Down local line was clear by 1900 and the Down main shortly afterwards at 1918. The Up main operative from 2045 the next day. Some disruption still remained as trains were unable to call as the platforms were still blocked by debris: in consequence a replacement bus service operated between Sydenham and New Cross Gate. Last to reopen was the Up local line from 26 June, from that date also services started calling again at Honor Oak and Brockley. Due to subway damage it was not possible to re-open the centre, Main-line, platforms at Forest Hill until 0630 on 23 July.

1944 - THE FLYING BOMBS

There is some slight confusion over the date of this next incident, although the location, the main line between East and South Croydon is not in doubt. According to 'London Main Line War Damage' an incident caused by high explosive occurred at 0040 on Saturday 25 March 1944. But according to the note accompanying the illustrations, these images are dated 23 May 1944. Whatever, enemy action has resulted in damage to the embankment and consequent undermining of the Down relief line. Whilst in the above view the illustration was of course taken to show work in progress towards the restoration of facilities, of almost as much interest is the cargo on the train cautiously passing alongside - clearly part military vehicles. Using the first date of 25 March as a starting point, all lines were reported as blocked in consequence of the HE attack. The local lines were cleared by 0435, the Up main at 1010 and the Down main at 1045 with a speed restriction of 15mph over each route. The Down relief reopened with a 5mph restriction at 0655 on 27 March. This latter restriction at least remained in force until 1600 on 12 April.

A closer view of the damage caused, fortunately not as bad as it might have been. The side of the embankment will be repaired and will then be stabilised. Perhaps surprisingly the signal gantry appears intact (the negatives do not have any more imagery of the actual signals upon them). In the lower two view, an EMU is seen approaching and then passing the scene of work.

Destruction at Hither Green on Friday 23 June 1944, following the explosion of two separate Flying Bombs, one at 0705 and the second at 0715. They fell one each side of the railway causing in official terms 'damage' to the station. In more detail the explosion blasted the Dartford Loop lines from Lee and also the Up through line. Cables and signalling were also cut. Despite the devastation visible, just two passengers and three members of staff were injured. Services were restored on the loop lines at 16.50 and on the Up main at 0810 the next day. (A separate report of the incident states two electric trains and a number of wagons in a siding were damaged.) The air raid shelters seen appear to have emerged relatively unscathed. The sidings at Hither Green had been attacked just a week earlier on the night of 15/16 June, on this occasion 'C' class 0-6-0 No. 1593 was damaged with six wagons derailed, 40 other wagons were damaged plus four brake-vans. Peripheral damage was also caused to doors and windows of various offices. All sidings were back in use by 2100. Despite the obvious damage to civilian housing, reports indicate just 14 people were killed by the V1 and later V2 offensive in the Hither Green and Grove Park areas.

Above - *Destruction in the Booking Office at Hither Green following the raid of 23 June 1944.*
Opposite - *The wrecked station canopy.*

A later V2 rocket attack at Hither Green Sidings in the early hours of 3 November 1944, resulted in the following formal summary. *"Referring to entries on the Railway Executive Committee (R..E.C). morning and evening reports of 3rd instant, I have to inform you that at 4.40 am on 3 November, there was a happening which caused a crater approximately 30 feet across and 20 feet deep in 'C' section on the down side at Hither Green Sidings, resulting in damage to sidings Nos. 1 to 7 inclusive in that sec-*

tion which, in consequence, had to be closed.
"It was also necessary to close 'B' section owing to the debris which was subsequently cleared and this section was reopened at 3.45 pm.

"Between 80 and 100 freight rolling stock vehicles sustained damage, whilst, in the up sidings, doors, windows and ceilings in Shunters Lobby, RCH Office, Police Office, Decontamination Room and Yard master's Office were damaged by the

blast, and in the Down sidings the Ladies Lavatory was destroyed.

"The down and up through and down and up local lines between Hither Green Sidings 'B' and 'C' signal boxes were closed for examination from 4.40 am to 5.43 am. There was no damage to these lines but all communication between 'B' and 'C' boxes was destroyed and traffic was worked on the time interval system until the restoration of telephone communication at 10.18 am. The block instruments were restored at 12.20 pm, and block bell communication on the up and down through lines at 11.05 am and on the up and down local lines at 1.30 pm.

"To assist the working during the operation of the time interval system between Hither Green 'B' and 'C' boxes, the morning business period through services between Bromley North and Cannon Street and Charing Cross were suspended, and a shuttle service instituted between Bromley North and Grove Park.

"As regards freight services, a number of freight trains from Hither Green were cancelled and exchange traffic form the LNE (GN section) and LMS (Midland section) was diverted to Herne Hill, Blackheath, and Bricklayers Arms, until the opening of 'B' section.

"There were casualties amongst the staff as follows:-

Guard Sutton (Hither Green)	Injury to right leg.
Shunter Wynne (Hither Green)	Head and leg injuries.
Driver Latter (Tonbridge)	Slight injuries.
Driver Aubrey (Hither Green)	Slight injuries.
Shunter Woodnott (Hither Green)	Slight injuries.
RCH Number Taker Grey	Slight injuries.

"All the foregoing were conveyed to Lewisham Hospital but only Guard Sutton was detained at the time. Shunter Wynne, upon subsequently attending hospital was also detained.

Platforms 1 and 2 at Victoria (Eastern) after a V1 fell on to and set fire to the General Offices at 0156, 25 June 1944. Extensive damage was caused to the offices and the Royal Waiting Room was destroyed. EMU unit No. 1475, and possibly some others was reported damaged. Not surprisingly the station was closed, four being killed and 16 seriously wounded, including two members of staff. Seven members of staff were reported as missing although one subsequently turned up at home. The gruesome toll continued with two bodies that were unidentified and four others, all passengers, who were later identified. One of those hospitalised later died from injuries. Meanwhile on the ground, the Central Section platforms were closed for examination until 0350, platform Nos. 4-8 were back in service at 0500 and platform 3 at 0925 on 27 June. Nos 1 and 2, which been nearest the blast were in operation again from 0400 on 13 July.

***Left** - A close up of the damage to the roof.*

A close study of the associated images reveals a YMCA Forces Canteen and Rest Room on Platform 1. The presence of what are obviously milk churns will also be noted. In the street scenes it is definitely a question of 'the morning after the night before' as the first steps are taken towards the clear up and which includes the presence of a mobile crane. In the lower left image the pantechnicon has clearly been caught in the blast, odd items of furniture visible from the blown out top of the bodywork. The drum nearer the camera carries the inscription 'Pool Derv Fuel'.

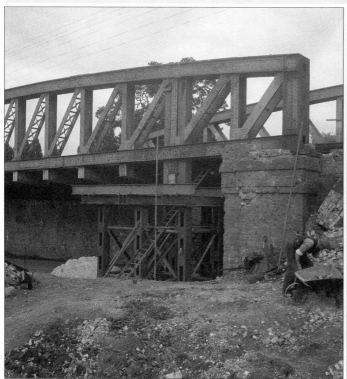

This page - *The effect of bombing - type unknown, on the bridge carrying the Brighton main line over the A23 south of Croydon. Reported as on 29 June 1944, there is some doubt as to the accuracy of the date although certainly there was damage to Southern Railway property at Ladywell, Beddington Lane, Wimbledon and Coombe Road at that time. In the views seen, damage to a supporting pier has necessitated a temporary structure to support the bridge itself.*

Opposite page - *At 1230 on Saturday 1 July 1944 a V1 landed on Messrs Lovibonds's brewery on the Up side of the railway at Greenwich. Not surprisingly the bombing rendered the brewery out of action whilst the station and platforms were extensively damaged. Windows were smashed in the 1148 EMU ex-Cannon Street. Five persons, including the station booking clerk were seriously injured, many others less so. Although specific casualty numbers are not given, the death toll from the V1 offensive for London and the South East during July 1944 was some 2,500 souls. After the station buildings had been made safe the lines re-opened at 1730 but Greenwich station was closed until 3 July.*

Above - Reported as clearing debris from the line near the station.

A bad day at Streatham Junction South* - but compare it also with the terrible destruction of domestic property alongside the line - seen opposite. The official record of this V1 attack was that it occurred, according to the SR at 0435 - according to civilian records a few minutes later, no matter, what is surprising is that despite the damage seen just four houses were demolished although it was admitted there was severe damage to surrounding property. The device had exploded in the vicinity of No. 40 Besley Street resulting also in all lines bring blocked by debris as well as the damage to the signal box seen. The Mitcham Junction lines were re-opened by 1010, and the Tooting lines shortly afterwards at 1025. (In the view opposite several signal arms are missing, no doubt those damaged already removed and awaiting replacement.)

Unfortunately there was also extensive damage to rolling stock at the nearby Eardley sidings. This amounted to 51 vehicles, including five Pullman cars and two complete Casualty Evacuation Trains. Telecommunications were reported as destroyed, but clearly repairs were again rapid, for despite the damage seen, normal working was resumed just 13 hours later at 1730.

* (The record of the event at this location refers to it as having occurred at 'Streatham South Junction'.)

The timber station at West Dulwich after a V1 attack at 1704 on Sunday 6 August 1944. Despite the device having reported as fallen directly on to the Down side buildings and set the structure on fire, the damage is perhaps not as bad might have been expected. An unspecified number of passengers in the waiting room at the time were injured. A train (not detailed) was also damaged. The station was closed and the line closed between Herne Hill South, Sydenham Hill and Penge East. The route was restored at 1559 on the following day. In the view above, at least two women workers are involved in conducting repairs, the station re-opened just three days later from 0400 on 9 August. (Nearby Sydenham Hill was hit by a similar device six minutes after the attack at West Dulwich. The bomb fell between the platform and tunnel and struck the rear of the 1654 EMU from Victoria to Orpington causing both damage and injury to passengers. The force of the blast also blew a tree across the tracks. Apart from the necessary temporary closure of the line, services were diverted via Nunhead and a shuttle service introduced between Shortlands and Penge East.)

There were two flying bomb incidents in the vicinity of Crystal Palace in two days (there had been an earlier one on 11 July 1944 as well). On 9 September, a V1 struck Palace Square, at 1810 ,on 11 September the impact was in Annerley Road immediately outside the station. It was later reported that on one of these occasions people had heard the engine cut-out and were attempting to make for the cover of a basement shelter, although regretfully not all succeeded. As well as the station - see also page 4 of Part 1 of this series - 18 shops in Station Road were demolished and there was also a fire. A further eight shops and seven houses were severely damaged, whilst a further 84 houses suffered slight damage over a wide area. The Paxton Arms Public House was badly damaged and did not re-open until 1955 - one of the rescuers from that day in 1955 the first to take a drink upon reopening. The views were taken on 12 September.

The last incident of damage that has been located as being recorded on film was at St Mary Cray on 8 March 1945. Two months later it would all be over, so far as Europe was concerned at least, although after 8 March there were still to be rocket attacks on the SR until the 26 March. In the incident depicted, a rocket has exploded in the Up side station approach at 0440 damaging the station buildings and severing the HT cables supplying the live rail. As a result there was no power between St Mary Cray - Swanley and Dunton Green - Sevonoaks. The lines were closed for examination until 0550 with power being reinstated at 0620. Unfortunately telecommunications damage also meant there was contact between the signal boxes at St Mary Cray Junction and St Mary Cray. Consequently with power

restored, trains were reinstated using 'Time Interval Working'. This was continued until normal working was back in force at 1530 the same day.

Behind the scenes, on 14 September 1944, the SR Finance Committee had reported in summary on the effect of the V1 offensive to that time. So far there had been 490 incidents, half of which were in the London area over a period of just 78 days. This had resulted in 83 line blockages, all but one - the Down line at Charing Cross - having been cleared. Detail was also given with regard to casualties: 12 staff had been killed and 157 injured. The passenger count was 37 killed and 423 injured. It was noted that all these figures were higher than any of the other railways in the same period, including the London passenger Transport Board, and goes to show that the Southern Railway was truly on the front line in WW2.

75

No photographs of the Rainham incident have been located, but we do have these images of a V1 attack at Durnsford Road, Wimbledon, a few weeks earlier on 29 June 1944. At 1032 a flying bomb fell on an empty EMU in No. 1 carriage siding, the train was badly damaged and the motorman killed. (For details of the damaged stock, see table on page 36 of Part 2.) Two other staff were injured. The ramp at the west end of the flyover carrying the Up local line was also damaged, also the Down and Up Putney lines. Debris was strewn over all lines. The main Up and Down running lines were re-opened for steam services at 1230, and for electric traction at 1352. The Down local was in use again at 1550: the East Putney lines for steam at 1400, and electric trains at 1638. The Up local was restored with a 10 mph speed restriction at 1415 on 30 June. The temporary speed restriction was not withdrawn until 1600 on 22 September. No. 1 carriage siding was reopened at 1130 on 5 July. In summary it can be said that the through lines were in operation in three hours and the flyover in 27 hours.

THE SCENE BEHIND THE SCENE

The effect of enemy bombing on railwaymen, passengers and indeed general morale has been discussed many times. Sometimes though it was just an unfortunate set of circumstances, bad luck for one side - good luck to the other, which led to a specific situation. The consequences of this were examples of stoic actions by railwaymen - and others. Of no doubt there were countless examples of such behaviour, some perhaps recorded, possibly because of the magnitude of the accident and its ensuing aftermath, others quietly forgotten, the individuals themselves content to keep 'mum'.

Rainham, Kent, is just one example of action, consequence, and response, described initially (and with official sanction) by Bernard Darwin. "On August 16 (1944) a bomb (V1) was shot down: it fell on a bridge which carries the line over a country lane beyond Rainham Station, between Gillingham and Sittingbourne, and made a hole in it. Just at this moment a passenger train from Victoria was drawing near and the bomb fell twenty yards or so in front of it. The driver saw it coming and used his emergency brake, but he could not stop the train before the bridge. The engine was overturned, dragging the first two coaches with it, eight people were killed and sixteen seriously injured. (A list of the casualties is give at the end of this discussion topic). Some little while before something of the same kind had happened on another part of the line, with a luckier issue. A pilot who had helped to bring down a flying bomb was able to signal to the driver of a goods train* so that he could pull up a few yards short of a mass of rubbish thrown across the track."

* According to a report on the BBC website: http://www.bbc.co.uk/dna/h2g2/A51606894 , a WAAF survivor is of the opinion the accident to the passenger train was in fact caused by an RAF pilot who, in knocking the V1 off course, had to watch in horror as "...the V1, quite undamaged, flew, rather than plummeted, in an almost horizontal downward spiral towards the train as it approached the bridge at Oak Lane…...that poor man, the pilot! Circling round and round the crash-site in his plane, flying low, he must have felt so terrible".

Even allowing for the effect of time and memory, it might appear as if the accident at Rainham may have been the subject of some form of official cover-up as to the true cause, the story of the preceding goods train incident little more than invention, intended to divert attention to a, possible spurious incident. (In March 1943, 173 people were killed in a crush at Bethnal Green Tube Station. Although reported at the time, the location of the disaster was not made not public and the government took steps to suppress the full details no doubt for fear of public alarm.)

The following on the Rainham, Oak Lane Bridge incident, is reproduced from Ben Brooksbank's notes:

"In the late afternoon of Wednesday 16 August 1944, a V1 caused about the worst and most dramatic incident on the railways due to V-weapons and the circumstances deserve full description.

"The first 'bare-bones' report is of the 17 August, by the SR Traffic Manager, R M T Richards, at Deepdene to the General Manager, as follows:- "At about 4.50pm yesterday, as the 3.35 p.m. Victoria to Ramsgate, formed of 10 coaches and a van, was closely approaching underline bridge No. 181 between Rainham and Newington, a flying bomb destroyed the bridge leaving a gap in the line. The engine, No. 806 (King Arthur class), actually got over the gap but was apparently overturned by the first coach which became badly derailed at right angles to the line; the second and third coaches also became derailed.

"The train conveyed about 400 passengers. Seven passengers were killed, as was also Sub-Ganger Naylor; 15 passengers and a Permanent Way Inspector were seriously injured, whereas 21 passengers and an Engineer's Department Bridge Inspector were slightly injured. All the injured were taken to hospital. The Driver of the engine sustained shock and the Fireman cuts on the head.

"The uninjured passengers in the 3.35pm were conducted to the main road and conveyed to Newington Station by 'bus. The 3.15pm train Ramsgate to Victoria was terminated at Newington and this stock used to convey passengers to destination.

"At the time of the accident, the 3.15pm train from Ramsgate was approaching Newington, where all signals were off for the train, but fortunately the signalman there, who had heard the flying bomb, realised that something untoward might have occurred, and [he] immediately replaced his Up line signals to Danger and the train was brought to a stand. Appeal was at once made in this train for any doctors who might be travelling by it and as a result two doctors and some orderlies were taken to the site of the mishap, where it was found that other doctors were already on the spot and all possible help was being rendered.

"Both lines are still out of use and in the meantime 'bus services are in operation between Sittingbourne and Gillingham, calling at Rainham and Newington. Breakdown appliances including three heavy cranes, namely from Ashford, Bricklayers' Arms and Redhill, are engaged in re-railing operations. The Divisional Superintendent is arranging to hold a Joint Enquiry. The Chief Civil Engineer advises me that he does not anticipate that the lines will be cleared until late on Saturday night or on Sunday."
Signed: *R.M.P. Richards.*

With a temporary bridge, the lines were in fact open again in three days. As a vivid insight into railway operations and the actions taken when they were disrupted by a major and unusual wartime 'Incident', the bulk of the Special Report, written by the SR Eastern Division Superintendent, seems worth reproducing here, together with some of the affidavits of the men concerned, also letters from passengers[1] :- "3.35 P.M. VICTORIA TO RAMSGATE DERAILED BETWEEN RAINHAM AND NEWINGTON STATIONS, WEDNESDAY, 16/8/1944, OWING TO BRIDGE No. 181 (40M. 2CHS.) BEING DAMAGED BY ENEMY ACTION. Memorandum of Joint Enquiry held at Rainham on Friday, 18th August, 1944, which could not be finally completed owing to the Driver and Fireman of the derailed train being absent sick.

This page and opposite: Back in time to 1940, when on 15 October an unfortunate strike occurred on the power station at Durnsford Road. At 2215 high explosive struck, demolishing the west chimney stack and rendering half the boilers out of action. Eight staff were injured and the electric current supply to the Western section was cut off. Limited alternative supplies were obtained immediately with power generation partially restored by 16 October. It was to be 127 days before full power generation resumed, with, in the meanwhile, electric trains operating at reduced speed. An employee, Wilfred Cyril Smith, was subsequently awarded the George Medal for his actions that night. Details of his gallantry are not reported.

PRESENT:- Mr. P. Nunn, London East Division Superintendent (Chairman); Mr. H. Lelew, representing East Division Locomotive Running Superintendent; Mr. W.E. Hancox, representing Assistant Chief Engineer (S&T); Mr. H.E. Kemp, representing Chief Mechanical Engineer; Mr. R. Hamnett, representing Eastern Divisional Engineer.

DATE & TIME OF OCCURRENCE: At Bridge 181 rail over road at Oak Lane between Rainham and Newington stations, 1m.7chs. from Rainham Station and 1m 47chs. from Newington Station.

STATE OF WEATHER: Fine.

GRADIENT: 1 in 264 falling towards Newington.

PARTICULARS OF LINES BLOCKED: Up and Down Lines.

FORMATION OF TRAIN: 3.35 p.m. steam passenger train Victoria to Ramsgate; Driver Barnett, Fireman Humphreys, both Stewarts Lane; Guard Russell, Victoria. Engine No. 806 – "Sir Galleron", N15 Class 4-6-0, chimney leading, left-hand drive, weight 81t. 17c.; 6-wheeled tender, weight 41t. 5c, vacuum brake operating on coupled engine wheels and all tender wheels. Stock [from front to rear]: Corr. Thirds 1263 and 1836, Corr. Third Bke 4049, Corr. Third 2350, Corr. First 7663, Corr. Thirds 2349 and 2351, Corr. Third Bke 4048, Corr. Third (nondescript) 1301, Corr. Third Bke 3175, Luggage Van 2431: total weight of train 331 tons, length 651' 5", plus engine and tender 61' 5". All the vehicles [were] fitted with steel under-frames, wooden battens with steel panels. All passenger vehicles were auto-coupled excepting the rear two.

The train left Victoria for Ramsgate on time at 3.35 p.m. and maintained schedule to Chatham. It left Chatham at 4.36 p.m. (4 minutes late), the delay being caused by heavy parcels and mail traffic. It had clear signals through Rainham and the evidence available indicates that when the train was some 200 yards from Bridge No. 181 (Oak Lane) at 4.47 p.m. travelling at 50/55 mph a flying bomb fell on the Down side of the line at the foot of the brickwork of the bridge on the Rainham side. The explosion apparently caused some movement to the whole of the bridge and it is assumed that the passage of the engine and the leading bogie of the first passenger vehicle caused the bridge to collapse.

The evidence of the Guard indicates [that] an emergency application of the brake was made by the Driver, but at the moment it has not been possible to obtain the Enginemen's statements owing to the fact that they are now absent from duty suffering from shock. [See below]. The time intervening between the explosion and the engine reaching the bridge would be approximately 6 to 8 seconds and, therefore, the Guard had not too clear a recollection of what happened, as he himself and also the female travelling Parcels Porter who was with him were flung across the van and were momentarily dazed.

The engine and also the leading bogie of the front coach seem to have negotiated the bridge. The following six bogies, i.e. the rear bogie of the first coach, two bogies of the second coach, two bogies of the third coach and the leading bogie of the fourth coach fell into the gap created by the collapse of the bridge. The engine and tender took a right-hand turn, no doubt being affected by the derailment of the passenger stock, and turned completely over, coming to rest with the chimney, dome and cab embedded in the Up running line. The first two passenger coaches telescoped and suffered considerable damage, taking a left-hand turn in the direction of travel and coming to rest partially down the slope of the slight embankment. The third coach came to rest between the Down and Up lines. The fourth coach partly bridged the gap, the rear bogie being still on the rails. The remaining six passenger coaches and the luggage van were not derailed.

The evidence indicates that the permanent way, which had been walked over by the Ganger immediately prior to the passing of the train, was in good order. The signalling communications also were in good order; nothing was amiss with the train when examined by the Carriage & Wagon Department staff at Victoria prior to leaving, and in addition the bridge itself was up to a good standard of maintenance.

There were approximately 400 passengers in the train and Guard Russell states that there were sufficient seats for all, although a certain number of passengers were standing in the corridor as the weather was very hot. The loading was heavier in the rear coaches than in the front. There were 462 seats.

The bomb fell at 4.47 p.m. and the derailment occurred a few seconds later. Unfortunately 7 passengers lost their lives; a Sub-Ganger who was on the permanent way was also killed. Another person has since succumbed to injury whilst in hospital, but there is considerable doubt as to whether this person had travelled by the train.

The train was due to pass the spot at approximately 4.43 p.m. and had it not been for the delay at Chatham would have been clear before the bomb fell.

A Police Constable and an Air Raid Warden observed the falling of the bomb and were on the site within two minutes of the derailment. A telephone message was sent from the adjoining house to the Rainham Civil Defence Control, and by 5 o'clock 6 motor ambulances, each capable of taking 4 stretcher cases, 2 motor rescue vans, each containing a rescue party with equipment and 1 mortuary van, left immediately. These vehicles arrived at the site between 5.5 and 5.10 p.m.

The Station Master at Rainham, who heard the bomb fall, came out onto the platform, when he was informed by his Signalman that his train communication bells were down and he [the SM] thereupon hastened to the scene, arriving there at approximately 5.10 p.m. He was accompanied by the Ganger whom he had met and was just finishing the walking of his length. Prior to this, Fireman Evans, who resides close to Rainham Station, had heard the bomb fall and having a daughter living in the vicinity, mounted his bicycle and proceeded to the site. He was the first Company's servant, apart from the Guard of the train, to arrive on the scene, and found that rescue work had already started and was being, in his view, most efficiently carried out.

The Guard of the train had also gone from the van at the rear of the 8th vehicle, in which he was riding, to the front and also found that rescue work was proceeding.

Guard Loft was riding (passenger) in the front van of the third vehicle, and he was handing out the emergency equipment to the many Service people who were eager to render assistance. Loft them proceeded to the rear brake van in the 8th vehicle and obtained the emergency equipment from that van also.

The Station Master then observed Fireman Evans and asked him to examine the engine to see whether there was any danger of explosion; this examination was quickly performed by Evans and as in his view the fire in the furnace was likely to cause damage, he appealed to the N.F.S. Firemen, who were then on the site, to play onto the fire in the furnace, which they did, and quickly extinguished same.

Sergt. Braid of the Kent Constabulary, attached to Newington, together with our Station Master, Mr. Hall, very quickly organised the rescue work, and it has been ascertained that the first casualty was sent to the Casualty Clearing Station about 150 yards from the scene by 5.5 p.m., and the last had been removed from the train very soon after 5.30 pm.

By far the greater number of casualties were in the first and second vehicles, which were very badly telescoped.

Sergt. Braid has been asked if there was any shortage of efficient tools, and his reply was that the demand was well met bearing in mind the equipment brought by the rescue squads, but that he would like to have had a supply of morphine to administer to some of the passengers who were suffering greatly from the accident.

There is no doubt that the help rendered by the medical men, First Aid men, Service representatives and others on the train, also the Police, the Civil Defence and National Fire Service staff at Rainham, was admirably performed, and we have been unable to find that any complaint was made respecting the way in which the unfortunate people were dealt with.

Several of our Permanent Way staff were at the scene within a few minutes and rendered excellent service to the injured.

Steam cranes were asked for at 5.50 p.m. and an intimation was given that at least two 35-ton cranes would be required and one would have to work to the scene over the Down Road from Newington.

A special train of Engineer's workmen left Sittingbourne for the site at 6.46 pm. and these men assisted those already there to clear the lighter debris from the running lines. The heavy lifting was commenced early on Thursday morning.

Although the Fireman of the derailed engine had sustained several cuts, he at once proceeded to protect the Up Road and placed detonators on the line at the required distances, and then continued on to Newington, being met en route by a Porter at the latter Station.

The speed of the train immediately prior to the derailment was between 50 and 55 miles per hour, which is not excessive over the stretch of line in question.

The 3.15 p.m. Ramsgate to Victoria was due to pass the Bridge on the Up line at approximately 4.50 p.m. This train was offered to Porter (2) Acting Signalman Chambers by Sittingbourne Western Junction at approximately 4.50 p.m. Chambers offered the train to Rainham on receipt of the "Train Entering Section" signal from Western Junction, when he gave the "Call Attention" signal and then the "Is Line Clear?" signal. He states he obtained a "Free" on his Sykes' Instrument. He admits that he did not get the correct acknowledgment to the "Is Line Clear?" or the "Call Attention" signal, but merely obtained a click. Having obtained the "Clear" as he thought from Rainham, he lowered all the running signals for the Up Road, but having heard a bomb drop at approximately 4.47 p.m. and realising that the 3.35 p.m. ex-Victoria had not passed, he at once endeavoured to obtain telephonic communication with Rainham. This he could not do and he immediately then replaced his Up signals, and we are satisfied that the Distant signal had been replaced before the Driver of the Up train obtained a view of same.

Chambers realises now that he should have repeated the "Is Line Clear?" signal to Rainham and obtained a proper acknowledgment before lowering his signals, but was apparently misled by the freeing of the lock on the Sykes' Section Instrument.

It is thought that there was some failure in the apparatus, brought about by the wires being down at the scene of the derailment and it was an irregular contact which enabled him to pull his leading signal.

The Up train arrived at Newington platform at approximately 4.55 p.m. having first been stopped at the Home signal. Signalman Chambers, in the meantime, had sent Dock Porter Gillman to ascertain the state of the roads ahead, Gillman travelling by cycle in the Up side cess. After proceeding about a mile he met the Fireman of the derailed engine who gave him full particulars of the derailment, location *etc.*, when Gillman at once returned to Newington to phone the Civil Defence Centre to send Doctors, Nurses, Equipment *etc.*, to the scene at once.

I myself (Mr. Nunn) was travelling on the Up train and upon ascertaining from Gillman what had happened, I instructed the Guard to go through the train to ascertain if there were any Doctors or First Aid Workers on same that were prepared to go the scene and if so would they assemble by the engine. Two Doctors were discovered and two First Aid Workers.

The engine was detached and these four volunteers, together with the Fireman of the derailed engine and Mr. Nunn, travelled to the scene, a wrong line order having first been obtained from Signalman Chambers. It was found that by this time most of the casualties had been removed from the train and Mr. Nunn specially contacted Sergt. Braid and after a careful examination it was agreed that all the casualties had been removed, although as one of the helpers intimated he thought he had heard moans, a further search was made in the telescoped coaches, but the first view that all had been removed was confirmed.

The protection of the Up Road was duly carried out by the Fireman of the derailed engine who had sustained minor cuts, but he apparently did not make contact with the Guard of the train. When the Guard reached the Engine he was unable to see either of the Enginemen and immediately sent his Travelling Parcels Porter forward to protect the Up Road. The Guard himself returned to the rear and protected the Down Road, placing flags at the recognised distances.

CONCLUSION.

After having heard the evidence of all concerned, we are certain that the unfortunate mishap was not in any way due to anything wrong with the permanent way, bridge, signalling equipment, engine or stock and that the cause is attributable to the falling of the flying bomb.

We have been unable to obtain the evidence of the Driver and Fireman of the derailed train, but it would appear that the bomb fell on the Down side of the line adjacent to the brick support nearest to Rainham. The blast naturally affected the bridge, and the passage of the train immediately after probably brought down the superstructure.

Signed:- P. Nunn, London East Divisional Supt.; H. Lelew, for Eastern Divisional Locomotive Running Superintendent.; W.E. Hancox, for Assistant Engineer (S.& T.); H.E. Kemp, for Chief Mechanical Engineer; R.A. Hamnett, for Eastern Divisional Engineer.

An Appendix describes the 'Particulars of Re-Railing Assistance, Re-railments and Clearance of Lines', which can be summarised:- Requested at 17.50 (but message not received by Loco Dept. until 19.20), Ashford crane (working at Pluckley), left Pluckley 20.25, delayed at Ashford awaiting Guard and arrived at derailment at 03.15 (17/8); Bricklayers Arms crane (working at Chislehurst), left there 20.45, delayed at Ashford by enemy action (*see below*) and owing to hot box at Ramsgate awaiting Ashford Tool Van, arrived 05.25. The Brighton crane (working at Earlswood) was requested at 20.15, left Earlswood at 03.25 and arrived at derailment at 08.00. The Gillingham Tool Van was requested 18.00, left there 20.25 and arrived 21.15; the Faversham Tool Van was ordered by the Loco Department at 20.00, left at 22.40 and arrived at midnight. (Considerable congestion occurred at Ashford, as all freight traffic had to be diverted by this route).

The engine was re-railed at 10.00, Corridor-Third No. 2350 at 11.15, the tender at 14.00 (17/8); other derailed coaches were totally destroyed. The Up line was cleared 11.50, the Down line 13.30 on 19/8, both with 5 mph SpR.

The Driver and Fireman of the derailed express were both injured and unable to give evidence at the Joint Enquiry. Their written statements were as follows (slightly modified [2]):-
"Charles Barnett – Driver, attached to Stewarts Lane: age 61, service 43, driver 23 years.

I commenced duty at 2.15 p.m. on Wednesday 16th August 1944, at Stewarts Lane and after preparing the engine, left at 3.15 p.m. for Victoria, and then worked the 3.35 p.m. to Ramsgate, the engine being in good order.

We had a clear run as far as Rainham and shortly after passing Rainham Station, my hat was blown from my head and on looking out I saw a cloud of smoke in front of me. I at once closed the regulator and made an emergency application of the brake simultaneously.

I felt the engine turn over and [I] hung onto the reversing wheel and [it was then] that the injury to my right shoulder resulted. My Fireman, after wriggling from under a pile of coal, helped from the cab. He then went forward to protect the Up Road. My injury was causing me great pain. A Platelayer obtained a box on which I sat and whilst [I was] seated the whistle commenced to blow. I made an [unsuccessful] effort to reach the plunger, [but] the whistling ceased after the boiler pressure had escaped. After some minutes I asked the Platelayer whether he could help me reach the First Aid Post. He helped me down the embankment and an Army Despatch Rider then carried me down Oak Lane to the main road, where I was placed in a motor vehicle and taken to a First Aid Post at Rainham Schools. There I received attention from a Doctor and from there, together with my Fireman, was taken to the St Bartholomew's Hospital, Rochester. I was given further attention there and an X-ray was taken of my injured shoulder. After a time, I was informed by a Doctor that I had no bones broken, but he advised me to visit my local hospital next morning for attention. My Fireman and I were then taken by an improvised ambulance to Chatham Station, as I was anxious to get home, by some Rainham First Aid ladies, who placed us in a first class compartment on the 8.54 p.m. from Gillingham to Victoria.

I travelled from Victoria to Clapham Junction [in a brake van], where I changed into a train for Worcester Park; [My Fireman went home to Balham]. I arrived home at 12.45 a.m.

Fireman David Humphreys: age 42, service 25, fireman 24 years. I was Fireman to Driver Barnett on the 3.35 p.m. Victoria to Ramsgate on Wednesday 16th August 1944. We ran well to Rainham and when approaching what I now know to be Oak Lane Bridge, I was sweeping the footplate, after having attended to the fire. I felt some blast and then observed a large cloud of smoke in front of the engine. I immediately opened the dry sand valve and observed that the Driver, at the same time, made an application of his brake and also closed the regulator. The next thing I remember is being covered with coal on the right-hand side of the footplate, the engine having turned completely over. Driver Barnett was on top of me and we both endeavoured to wriggle free. After I got clear, which was before Barnett, I rendered assistance to Barnett and in answer to my query as to how he felt, he told me he was all right. I myself was bleeding badly from the wrist and also from minor cuts on the head.

I was then anxious to protect the Up Road knowing that a train was due to pass, but as our detonators were in the tender tool-box and were not obtainable, I proceeded towards Newington and came to a platelayers' hut. This was locked and I endeavoured to break it open but, at the same time, the Female Travelling Parcels Porter called me back and I obtained some detonators from her. I placed the detonators on the line at the proper distances and then proceeded towards Newington to acquaint the Signalman of what had happened. By chance I met two Army Officers who insisted on binding up my wrist, ... I [then] continued on my journey, meeting two Platelayers, one of whom was carrying a red flag. We then proceeded on towards Newington, when I met a Dock Porter from the latter Station who was riding a cycle. I gave him full details of what had happened and he at once returned to Newington to give the information. I then continued on to Newington where I went to the Signal Box and myself informed the Signalman of the situation.

I afterwards travelled on the engine of the 3.15 p.m. ex-Ramsgate back to the site, together with the Divisional Superintendent, two Doctors and two RAMC Orderlies. I endeavoured to find the Driver, and one onlooker intimated that he had passed away and had been taken to hospital. I was then conveyed by motor ambulance to the Rest Room at Rainham where I was pleased to find Driver Barnett, who however was in a somewhat dazed condition. We were both examined there and given attention. We then went to St Bartholomew's Hospital but were afterwards released and proceeded home. We were conveyed to Chatham Station by ambulance and two female assistants carried our bags and belongings ... to the Up train to Victoria at Chatham and placed us in a first-class compartment.

(Fireman Humphreys was awarded an Official Commendation).

George Russell, Guard, Victoria: age 43, service 27, guard 4 years.

We left Victoria right time, but were 4 minutes late leaving Chatham ... at 4.36 p.m. This delay was due to heavy platform work.

To the best of my recollection the train became derailed at 4.48 p.m. I had seen the Rainham Down Distant Signal in the "off" position and the next occurrence was the sudden stopping of the train. I am of opinion that an application of the brake was made by the Driver immediately he observed the explosion of the bomb. I at once left my brake, which was the fourth vehicle from the engine, and proceeded along the train, together with Mrs. Rose, the female who was assisting me with parcels and luggage. ... Sailors and others were alighting and going to the assistance of the injured in the front coaches. ... A woman called out from alongside the Up Road that the ARP authorities had already been phoned for.

Guard Loft was riding passenger in the front brake and ... was handing out the emergency equipment, including the medical case, extinguishers etc. ... and from the back brake. I at once went to the engine but could not see either of the crew, so I assumed that the worst had happened to them and sent my female assistant forward to protect the Up Road. I observed a member of the NFS working about the train, prior to my leaving to protect the Down Road. I should estimate that I left the scene within 5 minutes of the derailment and placed fog signals on the line at agreed distances. I then returned to the train, assisting as far as possible with the first aid work.

I heard of no complaint at all respecting delay to first aid work which I think was excellently performed by a large number of Police, First Aid Workers, Civil Defence Representatives and others who were then present. I should estimate that there was sufficient seating accommodation for all the passengers in the train, although, as is always the case, a certain number were in the corridor as the weather was extremely hot. The loading, in my view, was heavier in the rear coaches than in the front.

George White, Ganger: age 60, service 43, lengthman (Newington – Rainham) 26 years. I was walking my length at the time the derailment occurred and I estimate that I passed over Oak Lane Bridge at approximately 4.20 p.m. and found everything in order. When nearing Rainham Station I heard three flying bombs over-head, one of which was being attacked by one of our aircraft. At the same time I heard a bomb fall. The 3.35 p.m. Down passed me at Rainham Station and I estimated its speed to be between 50 and 60 miles per hour. I met Mr. Hall, the Station Master, who informed me that his communications were down and I proceeded with him in the direction of Newington.

When we arrived at the site of the derailment, assistance to the injured had already commenced and one of my own men was engaged on this work. After obtaining brief particulars I returned to Rainham Station to advise the Permanent Way Inspector at Sittingbourne of the derailment. I did this by means of the public telephone, afterwards returning to the site to assist generally.

I heard no complaints from the passengers and it seemed to me that the rescue work was being admirably carried out. … The motor ambulances were in Oak Lane and First Aid men were removing several of the wounded on stretchers. I was afterwards told by a man working in the adjacent orchard that the train was only about 200 yards from the point where the bomb fell demolishing the bridge.

Statements of Evidence were made also by other railwaymen involved: Signalmen Woodsell (Rainham) and Chambers (Newington), Dock Porter Gillman (Newington), Driver Shelvey (driving the Up express from Ramsgate), Guard Saunders (of the same train), Chief Lineman Bartholomew (Chatham) and by a Passed Fireman (John Evans) who was off duty in his garden nearby and hurried to help by bicycle.

Two handwritten letters by passengers preserved in the same file at the National Archive deserve quotation. Mr. H.W. Pendry of Leysdown (Isle of Sheppey) wrote to the SR General Manager (E.J. Missenden) on 18/8/44:-

"Dear Sir, My son was a passenger on the 3.35 p.m. from Victoria on the 16th inst. and am thankful to say he escaped any injury. He tells me that in his opinion the disaster was greatly diminished by the wonderfully quick action of the Driver in applying the brakes and in the few split seconds bringing the train to almost half speed. He understood the Driver and stoker were thrown clear and hopes both will soon completely recover and thought you might like to tell the Driver that his presence of mind and quick action undoubtedly saved many lives and reduced the damage caused by enemy action. I am, Yours sincerely, H.W. Pendry."

The other letter, written from Margate General Hospital to the Legal Adviser, Southern Railway, on 19/8/44 is of a different nature:- "Dear Sir, I was a passenger in the London to Margate train which was derailed at Newington on Wednesday afternoon, 16th August 1944 and I was travelling to Westgate on Sea. I was in the first coach behind the engine and approximately the fourth compartment. As I am a doctor I did not report my injuries at the scene of the accident. After resting for some time I continued my journey, from the scene of the accident to Sittingbourne Station in a van. Following about one and a half hour's wait there[3], by train to Westgate on Sea. On my arrival a doctor was called immediately, and exertion was causing an exaggeration of symptoms and he ordered my removal to hospital by ambulance. I am likely to be detained for some time yet. In view of this I should be glad if you could have my case put on the official list of those detained in hospital as a result of injuries received in the accident.

I enclose a medical certificate with details of my injuries. Thanking you in anticipation. Yours faithfully, Olga M. Sainsbury, L.R.C.P., M.R.C.S." The replies to these letters do not seem to be in the files.

However, preserved on file are replies from Sir Eustace Missenden to letters of sympathy evidently sent to him by his General Manager colleagues of the REC, Sir William Wood (LMSR) and Sir Charles Newton (LNER), thus:- "My Dear Wood, It was most kind of you to send me a letter of sympathy in connection with the Rainham accident and I much appreciate it. The train was travelling at about 65 m.p.h. when a "fly" bomb destroyed an underline bridge a few seconds before the train reached it. Curiously enough, the engine jumped the gap of 22 feet, taking the two leading carriages with it. These were seriously damaged, but I understand the buck-eye coupling on the vehicles which were stopped short of the bridge behaved magnificently and saved us from further casualties.
Yours sincerely, E.J. Missenden."

The final items of correspondence to be mentioned are a letter to Missenden from an army Captain, this and the subsequent reply describe well the actions of the injured fireman.

"Dear Sir, My Adjutant (Capt J M Roberts) and myself were witnesses to the terrible accident to the 3.25 train from London , which occurred between Rainham and Newington at about 4.55 pm on Wednesday 16 August 1944. We would both like to bring to your notice, the extreme devotion to duty of the Fireman of that particular train.

On going on the line ourselves to see what assistance we might be able to give, we found ourselves about 200 yards on the Newington side of the accident. The fireman had extricated himself from the engine, and was running down the track, dazed and bleeding from cuts, in addition to being covered in oil and water. This was within a few minutes of the accident. We tried to stop him, but his chief concern was (a) to stop the up train which he said was due at any moment and (b) first aid kit for the injured. We managed to persuade him to at least have one of his cuts bandaged, and off he went.

This action was no doubt a duty on his part, but we felt we would like to make this comment, and offer praise for his action in view of the terrible conditions of the accident, and his first thought for others.
We did not ask his name other than the fact he was the fireman.
Captain Edward Marsh."

THE SCENE BEHIND THE SCENE

The reply from Missenden, dated 21 August, read, "Dear Sir, I have received, and very much appreciate, the letter of 17 instant signed by yourself and Captain J H Roberts.

The fine spirit and devotion to duty of the Fireman of the train which met with such an unfortunate accident at Rainham last Wednesday has already been brought to notice and you may rest assured that it will not be overlooked.

The man concerned is at present suffering from shock but I understand is making satisfactory progress.
Yours sincerely - EJM.

Captain Edward Marsh
L.A.C.
Home Guard, 27th (K.E.) Bri.,
221, Maidstone Road,
ROCHESTER, Kent.

What was clearly not said was already Missenden had been made party to some disturbing news, for on 18 August, a letter marked 'Secret' was sent by him to Col. A Trench at the Ministry of War Transport. The 'secret' designation hiding the grim truth - now publicly revealed 60 years later. The outline facts of the accident, as related by Missenden, need not be repeated again, but more importantly the letter did contained a damming statement, "It appears that at about 4.50 pm, as the train in question was closely approaching underline bridge No.

181.......a flying bomb was shot down destroying the bridge and breaching the track.....as soon as further information is available you shall have it."

1 - Preserved at National Archives. Rail 648/92.
2 - Almost word-for-word, so maintaining most of the rather stilted language.
3 - Actually, it was about half an hour!

Fatalities:
AB Charles W Cummins - RNB Chatham
AB Albert E Eley - HMS 'Queen Elizabeth'
Frank Albert Snazel - Leonard Road, Beckenham
Pte. Jeffrey Herbert Gallop - Whitstable Road, Faversham
Mrs Ivy Maud Smith - Herne Bay Raod, Swallowcliffe
Pte. V B Martin - ATS of Bowers Road, Shoreham
Arthur Edward Naylor - Truston Road, Rainham
One female - unidentified.

The SR Traffic Manager, R M T Richards, later recommended that Fireman (Acting driver) J C A Evans, Dock Porter R J Gillman, Guard W S Loft be awarded a letter of thanks and £2 gratuity each. Richard commented that at that particular time. 30 August, both the Driver and Fireman were still on sick leave and would themselves be the subject of some form of award later.

Picking over the debris at Purley, 18 August 1940. See also page 47 of Part 1. (The twin stripes on the arm of the policeman may well indicate the temporary rank of 'Acting Sergeant'.)

THE AIR RAID AND OCCURENCE LOGS

The Southern Railway maintained a record of occurrences during WW2 in a series of log books based on the respective divisional boundaries as well as a general record. Set out below are a few examples from each, combined to give a flavour of what it might have been like 'on the ground'. It must be stated this is a representative selection only for one particular area, and does not constitute a full record of everything that might have taken place even on the dates given.

30 November 1940 (6.10 pm to 1.15 am.)	Northam Station	HE bomb exploded in Booking Hall causing considerable damage to Booking Office and station footbridge.
	Northam Yard	Eight wagons burnt out.
1 December	Southampton Docks	Telephone distribution room destroyed by fire and some 500 lines radiating there from out of order. Numerous cables destroyed. The following buildings were gutted by fire: Transit sheds 14, 15, 16, 20, 21, 26, 27, 45 and 50. Warehouses 'M' and 'N', General Stores, Kings Warehouse, Fire Station, Control Centre and several buildings leased to tenants. Damage caused to Sheds 41, 44, 102, 106, 108 Grain Conveyor and Ship Repairing Works.
1 / 2 December	Southampton Docks	Ranks Mill and buildings leased to tenants gutted by fire during the night.
	Between Totton and Marchwood	Line blocked. Clear 2.30 pm 2 December. (Cause of blockage not stated.)
	Bevois Park	Four wagons burnt out.
1 / 2 December.	Between Southampton Central and Millbrook.	All lines blocked. Down and up through clear 5.00 pm, 2 December.
	Southampton Central	Goods Shed and signalling gear damaged by HE and incendiary bombs during the night.
2 or 3 December	Between Hythe and Marchwood	Two HE bombs caused slight damage to Nos. 13 and 14 down departure roads and No. 7 new siding.
3 December	Whilst damping down a fire caused by enemy action, he fell over some broken telephone wires.	D E Dones - deep incision from base of thumb to wrist.
5 December 7.30 pm.	Fratton	Goods Shed and East Signal box damaged by HE bombs at 7.30 pm. Damage also caused to coal crane, coal trucks and five engines at Loco Depot. Fireman fatality injured. Driver, two Firemen and Engine Cleaner injured. F Jarrett - Driver - Head injuries and shock. H Hillier - Fireman - Fatality H Oxford - Fireman - Shock, scalp injury middle of forehead. F Cox - Crane Driver - Chin cut and shock C W Cornwall - Driver - Metal splinters in lower part of body. E Dollery - Fireman - Suspected fracture of both legs. G H Moody - Cleaner (Acting Fireman) Metal splinters in all parts of head and leg.
5 December 8.00 pm	Fratton	Nos. 5 and 14 sidings damaged and out of use. Traffic Foreman and Shunter injured. Sidings restored for use 12.00 noon 7 December. R Webb - Lacerated scalp wound, penetrated wound in right side of thorax. W White - Stn. Foreman - Right hand lacerated by falling glass and slight shock.
5 December 8.00 pm	Cosham	Goods Shed and wagons damaged by HE bomb. Windows of station premises, signal box and coaching stock also damaged.

5 December 7. 50 pm	Between Havant and Portsmouth Harbour	Lines closed at 7.50 pm owing to failure of all communication, track circuits and points. Trains terminating at Havant and Fareham and bus services arranged as necessary. Signalling restored at 10.40 am at Portsmouth and at Fratton at 4.10 pm, 6 December. Down line reopened 9.47 am. Up line at 10.40 am. Both lines between Fareham and Portsmouth reopened at 1115 am, 6 December.
5 December 6.45 pm	Between Ryde Esplanade and Ryde St Johns Road	Both lines blocked. (Engine of 6.35 pm train Ryde Pier Head to Ventnor derailed). Down main clear 11.30 pm and Up line and Down loop line clear 9.00 am 6 December.
9 March 1941	Portsmouth Harbour	Jetty and S.S. 'Portsdown' slightly damaged by explosion of HE bomb. F E Cottrell, deckhand on P S 'Sandown': inflammation of eyes. R O Davies, fitter on P S 'Merstone': burns on face, arms and legs.
10/11 March 1941	Portsmouth & Southsea	Station buildings damaged and windows broken by explosion off Company's property. Refreshment Room slightly damaged by incendiary bomb. Four coaches slightly damaged. Roadway leading to Portsmouth Harbour station damaged by bomb. All traffic suspended during the raid between Havant, Fareham and Portsmouth. Telephone communication between Fareham and Cosham and between Fareham and Fort Brockhurst destroyed.
	Between Fratton and Portsmouth & Southsea	Down relief line and down siding, down and up main lines blocked. Up clear 11 March, down main clear 3.15 pm 12 March, down relief and down siding clear 13 March.
	Between Fort Brockhurst and Gosport	Single line blocked. Clear 11 March.
	Gosport	Station buildings including Station Master's house gutted by fire.
	Fort Brockhurst	Platform at Air Ministry siding damaged and three wagons derailed.
11 March	Green Lane Crossing, Fratton	Down and Up lines and down siding damaged. Up line clear 11 March and Down line clear, 3.15 pm, 12 March.
11 /12 March	Between Green Lane Crossing and Fratton	Down and Up lines at Honeyfield Bridge blocked. (Subsidence at site of damage.)
11 / 12 March	Nr. Copnor Bridge	Whilst proceeding to examine the line, W T Collins was struck by splinters from a bomb. Contusion to right abdomen and bruising to upper right arm.
11 March, 10 15 pm.	Southampton Docks.	One siding in Empress Yard damaged and a number of trucks on an adjacent siding derailed by two bombs.
12 March, 9 55 pm.	Southampton Docks	Two HE bombs fell on the power house and boiler house of Messrs. Harland & Wolff main works causing considerable damage. E Kitcher, employee of Harland & Wolff, bomb splinters in right leg, thigh and buttocks.
13 March, 8.41 pm.	Between Haslemere and Liphook.	Both lines blocked. Up cleared at 12.20 am, Down line cleared at 4.25 am 14 March.

Above - *To accompany the preceding Air Raid and Occurrence Logs, this is an additional image of the damage at Southampton but slightly later than referred to - 8 July 1941. (See also page 91 of Part 1.) Enemy action has caused damage which has in turn created an obstruction to the Up main line between Southampton Tunnel and Tunnel Junction. The wagon is noted as bearing the inscription 'Empty to Eastleigh Ballast Hole'. At this stage all effort would appear to undertaken by muscle power alone. Reports indicate there were three fatalities as a result of this raid - but in the Millbrook area of Southampton, some distance from that seen.*

Opposite - *Inside Nine Elms probably at the time of the official inspection. The engine on the right was (is) 4-6-0 No. 852 'Sir Walter Raleigh', severely damaged, but subsequently repaired. (See also pages 60 / 61 of Part 1, and Nos. 72 - 80 of Part 2.)*

THE DESTRUCTION OF NINE ELMS

The destruction at Nine Elms has been seen in photographic form in both Part 1 and 2. However, recently unearthed is a copy of a report of 8 October 1940 describing the effect of the raid of just over a week earlier which resulted in the destruction of T14 No. 458. The writer is not recorded, but it may well have been Missenden. "On the evening of 8 October, I accompanied Mr Bulleid the Chief Mechanical Engineer, to inspect the bomb damage at this depot, which is the largest on the system and accommodates 119 engines.

"An HE bomb (presumably 250 kilo) fell at 1.55 am on 30 September and hit tender engine No. 458, T14 class, 4-6-0 type, (of which there are 10 in all) when standing in the shed at the west end.

"The bomb struck the top of the boiler just behind the tube plate of the smoke box. It apparently passed straight through the boiler and exploded in the pit underneath. The engine was wrecked, derailed, and leaning on one side. The boiler plate was torn away from the tube plate at the joint; the tubes and superheaters were flattened and blown outwards; the frame on the nearside was torn nearly in two. A piece of the nearside tyre of the trailing bogie axle was broken, and the offside wheel was torn off the same axle.

"The tender had been recovered and was undamaged; but the only way of dealing with the engine was to cut it up for scrap, and that is in hand. It is an awkward job without an overhead crane, particularly as the engine is not resting on its wheels.

"The whole of the timber, glass, slates, asbestos smoke ducts, etc., throughout this big shed were blown away, but that may have been partly done by previous bombs. Steps have been taken to cover with felt the portion of the roof over machines, shops, stores, etc.

"Two pits in one corner of the shed had been transformed into shelters, the cover of sleepers and sand being carried by concrete walls on each side of the pits.

"The depot is only about half a mile from Battersea Power Station and the Gas Works, and Mr Maitland informed us that up to date there have now been five attacks, including the one under report:-

10 September.
14 September - An HE hit the shed near the west wall and the shelter, doing a good deal of damage to the building; a number of oil bombs also fell on the year and one hit a coal stack.
16 September
25 September - Ten incendiary bombs
30 September - As reported.

As a result of these raids, no less than 40 enginemen and other staff at Nine Elms have lost their homes.

"I understand that the Railway Construction Troops did excellent work in rapidly clearing the shed of the mass of wreckage from the roof.

"Mr Bulleid informed me that up to date, besides the engine in question which had bene destroyed, four have been badly damaged and 26 slightly damaged out of a total stock of 1,820 engines."

SEPTEMBER 1940

A second, slightly earlier, report from the same file describes an inspection made in part of the London area. It deals with bomb damage between Clapham Junction and Waterloo, again, the identity of the writer is not given. "I made an inspection with Mr. Ellson, the Chief Engineer on 20 September 1940. A DA hit No. 5 up platform on the night of 14 September which exploded on 16 September, forming a crater in the track and blowing out a proportion of the station building; it was made good and the road ready fro traffic within 24 hours.

"The line could not, however, be opened due to another DA on the Down local at Pouparts Junction which dropped at the same time; but it was not exploded until 5.00 pm on 19 September at the second attempt, little damage having resulted. It had penetrated 27 (?) feet, and I gathered that the Bomb Disposal Squad had been working with it all the time. Two rakes of coal wagons had been placed as a screen on 19 September. The Up and Down main lines were opened at 9.00 am on 19 September, and the locals were due to be opened about noon on 20 September after some ballast had been brought in. A big gang of men were on the job and were complimented by Mr. Ellson: a train arrived to roll out the track while we were there.

"Mr Ellson referred to the difficulties being experienced with regard to diagnosing DA bombs, much time having been wasted on going round each site and in most cases coming to the conclusion that a DA did not exist. Colonel Waghorn has been most helpful in lending two officers to act as liaison with London East Division, without encroaching on the duties of the Bomb Disposal Officers.

"Up trains were passing between 10.30 am and 11.00 am very lightly loaded.

"Clapham Junction 'A' Box was just missed when two bombs fell only some 50 yards north of, and adjacent to, this box.

They did terrific damage to the neighbouring thickly populated houses and formed two very large craters. Presumably they were at least 500 kilos, but this important box was undamaged.

"Colonel Hall's staff were much praised by the Traffic Inspector who took us round. He seemed more impressed with the way all this staff had been repairing signalling etc, than with anything else.

"The third bomb in this vicinity had fallen on the middle siding and had broken the crown of the arch, shattering two piers. The Up Windsor and Kensington arrival and departure roads were affected. Lieut. Jones with some 20 carpenters and 20 mates of the 158th Company were at work, timbering being carried out on the three spans (25 to 30 feet) affected. The baulks used were 14" x 14", uprights being put in with a transom and three struts on the top of each rail. Notwithstanding this very heavy under-pinning, which was being carried out very well, Mr Ellson feels that it is necessary to fill up the three arches with Meldon sand and block up the ends flush with heavy concrete walling. After packing the sand tight, it will be grouted and the timbers will then be buried, making a permanent repair; he thinks this will be quicker in the long run, and the additional delay to re-opening, on account of the filling in of the sand should not, he estimated, amount to more than three or four days.

"Russell Street Bridge, carrying the LBSCR over the LSWR. A bomb hit the end post of the main girder on 14 September and shattered the bedstone, destroying the bearing. The brickwork had to be rebuilt with a stool under the second post, packing tight with iron wedges. The Up main and Down local remained available into Victoria, and the Up local and Down main were returned to traffic again on 17 September. Another bomb nearby went through the decking, luckily missing the main girders."

Two additional views showing the damage to the Up Windsor and Kensington arrival / departure roads at Clapham Junction. One of the destroyed arches is illustrated in close up. See also page 63 of Part 1.

RURAL SUSSEX: 3 July 1940

ENEMY ACTION ON THE SEAFORD BRANCH

"At 5.43 pm on the 3 July, the 5.37 pm train from Seaford to Haywards Heath was attacked by an enemy aeroplane, and the following is a comprehensive narrative of the circumstances. The exact location was 340 yards the Newhaven side of Bishopsdown Beach Halt, the weather was fine and visibility was good. The service consisted - Leading Coach: Brake 3rd No. 6934, Rear Coach: Composite No. 2187, Engine: D1 class No. 2244 (propelling). The train crew were Guard: E H Batchelor, Brighton, Driver: C H Pattenden, Tunbridge Wells West , Fireman: F S Cox, Tunbridge Wells West. At the time a 'Yellow' - Preliminary Caution was in force, having been received at 4.03 pm. The 'White' - Cancel Caution, was received at 6.34 pm.

"On the day the 5.37 pm Seaford to Haywards Heath push-and-pull service left Seaford right time and there were only five passengers in the train.

"The schedule is a non-stop from Seaford to Newhaven Town and the journey was proceeding normally under clear signals. Guard Batchelor was riding in the leading (driving) compartment of the first coach. Driver Pattenden was at the controls on the left-hand side facing direction of travel, and Guard Batchelor was standing on the opposite (right-hand) side whilst a good lookout was maintained by both men.

"When the train reached a point 340 yards on the Newhaven side of Bishopstone Beach Halt, steam having already been shut off and speed reduced to about 15 mph preparatory to negotiation of the curve and junction at Newhaven Harbour, an enemy aeroplane approached from the sea in a SE - NW direction, and when crossing the line at an angle of about 60°, dropped seven bombs in quick succession.

"The first bomb fell twenty-two yards short of the Up line, outside the boundary fence, the second ten yards beyond the Down line, demolishing the boundary fence for a distance of some 27 feet, whilst the third, fourth, fifth, sixth and seventh bombs fell at respective distances of about 20 yards, 68 yards, 200 yards, 210 yards and 350 yards further over. Craters about five feet in diameter and three feet deep were formed in each case.

"Neither the Driver nor the Guard appears to have seen the aeroplane approach, and the sound of it was nullified by the noise of the train, but the explosions took place in quick succession and the detonations assumed the character of a multiple report.

"Bomb splinters struck the train and extensive shattering of glass ensued. The Driver and Guard were both struck by fragments, the Guard being knocked over on to the driving compartment floor while the Driver fell forward over his controls in an unconscious condition. The train came to a stand immediately beyond Newhaven Harbour Up Home Signal through fracture of the vacuum pipe and brake cylinders on the rear coach.

"On recovering himself, Guard Batchelor realised at once that the Driver was very seriously hurt , and decided to get the train to Newhaven Harbour as soon as possible. He accordingly put on his steel helmet and proceeded to walk around the train in order to ascertain what had befallen the passengers and the Fireman, and whether any vital damage had ensued either to the train or the permanent way.

"Fireman Cox was uninjured, however and had actually proceeded forward to see how the Driver had fared, giving minor first-aid to a passenger in the meanwhile. He and the Guard consulted together and after making the driver as comfortable as they could and laying him down on the driving compartment floor, it was agreed that the journey should be continued at once.

"At this juncture firing was heard overheard and passengers in the train leaned out enquiring what they should do. Guard Batchelor instructed them to keep well inside and lie down, which advice was obeyed at once, and he and the Fireman took cover themselves for a few moments until the firing appeared to recede. The Fireman then released the automatic brake (which operation was rendered difficult as a result of the damage which had occurred) and the journey was resumed under hand-brake. As a precautionary measure the Guard exhibited a red flag from the off side of the driving compartment in order to stop any movement approaching on the down line, as it was not known at the moment whether any damage had ensued to the permanent way further back.

"Motions were made to the Signalman when approaching Newhaven Harbour Box, but the train was waved forward, arriving at the platform at Newhaven Harbour at 5.55 pm.

"It should be mentioned at this point that the incident came under the immediate notice of Signalman G Ketchell, who was on duty at Newhaven Harbour Box, and the opportunity was taken to send the 'Obstruction Danger' signal to Seaford and to Newhaven Town 'B' at once. An acknowledgement was received from the latter only, however, as the explosion broke 12 telegraph and telephone wires and all railway communication with Seaford was cut off.

"On arrival of the train at Newhaven Harbour, First Aid attention was forthcoming at once under the leadership of Dock Porter Ince, and Medical Assistance was given by Major Fleming RAMC and Flight-Lieut Cunningham, RAF Medical Officer. It is regretted however, that Driver Pattenden succumbed to his injuries before he could be conveyed to Hospital. He was 59 years of age.

"It may be noted that Guard Bachelor, having felt something jagged between his underclothing and skin, retrieved a piece of metal about 2½ inches length and 1¼ inches wide and it transpired that this had penetrated his clothing and caused a somewhat severe flesh would. Bandages were supplied at once by the First Aid and Medical Personnel and the injured man was then despatched by Ambulance to Hospital in Newhaven where five stitches were put in the wound. Subsequent to this it was considered advisable to send him by Ambulance to the County Hospital at Brighton where he was x-rayed and underwent a minor operation with a local aesthetic. He was discharged from

Hospital at Brighton later in the evening, and arrived home at 9.30 pm where at the time of writing (10 July) he is still in bed and under surveillance of his own Doctor. Actually Batchelor was found to have sustained two small wounds in the neck and these were dressed by his Doctor at home.

"Reverting to the arrangements made at Newhaven, the train had of course, sustained very extensive superficial damage and the engine minor damage, and was shunted away immediately, the remainder of the trip being cancelled. It was assumed that the permanent way at the site of the attack would have suffered damage and the block imposed by Signalman Ketchell was accordingly maintained, a shuttle service being instigated between Lewes and Newhaven Town, and passengers for the Seaford Branch conveyed by (ordinary) Southdown Motor 'bus services.

"Porter Cutler and a Dock Porter walked down to the spot and reported that the line appeared un damaged, and an engine was then run through to Seaford for testing purposes and also to confirm that the Juniors on duty at Bishopstone Beach Halt and Bishopstone were unhurt. In the meantime a technical inspection was made by Permanent Way Inspector Jennings and it was possible to run an engine and brake from Newhaven to Seaford at 7.34 pm, returning thence with parcels traffic at 8.06 pm. A testing trip with an electric train was then run from Seaford at 8.24 pm returning from Newhaven harbour at 8.38 pm, this journey and the two preceding ones being run under the 'time interval' system.

"Block working was restored on the Down line at 8.15 pm and on the Up line at 8.35 pm after which normal running of passenger services was resumed.

"In conclusion it is desired to place on record the prompt and helpful action of all concerned, and the following in particular, viz: -

1 - Guard Batchelor, who though rather badly injured, continued duty and acted with promptitude, arranging for the train to be brought in to Newhaven Harbour, and Fireman Cox who likewise acted promptly in giving assistance, releasing the automatic brake and driving the train to Newhaven harbour under the hand brake.

2 - Mr G Hollands, Traffic Assistant to Divisional Marine Manager.

3 - Dock Porter Cutlor, who acted under Mr Holland's instructions.

4 - Major Fleming, RAMC and Ft. Lt. Cunningham RAF Medical Officer Newhaven, who rendered medical assistance.

5 - Dock Porter Ince - who was in charge of the Company's First Aid contingent.

6 - Signalman G Ketchell, Newhaven Harbour Box, who blocked the line immediately.

Further the conduct of the passengers in the train appears to have been exemplary.

A later SR report afforded clarification of certain issues, namely that several bomb fragments pieced the glass and driving end of the leading vehicles, it was these that had fatally wounded the Driver and injured the Guard. These came from the first of the falling bombs. The Fireman on hearing this first bomb drop lay flat on the cab floor. Both the Fireman and Guard later taking shelter beneath the train as the bombs continued to fall when both were by then on the ground. All five train passengers were injured, two of them children aged 1yr and 4 yrs. Both had cuts. Fireman Cox was later awarded a medal for meritorious service.

Driver Pattenden was reported not to have been wearing his steel helmet, had he have been it was considered his injury might not have proved fatal. The suggestion was made from the Locomotive Running Department at Tonbridge that an instruction be issued that helmets be worn whenever there was an air raid warning in place, regardless of the status of the warning. It is not known if this was actioned.

ELTHAM (WELL HALL) 14 NOVEMBER 1944

"Referring to the entry on the R.E.C. evening report of the 14th instant, I have to inform you that there was a 'happening' at 8.40 am on the 14 November, which occurred off the Company's property about 200 yards from Eltham (Well hall) station on the up side of the line, and damage to the roof, windows and doors of the station buildings and signal box was caused by the blast.

"The 8.18 am electric train from Barnehurst to Cannon Street comprised of eight caches (Unit No. 1478, Trailer set No. 99 and Unit No. 1413), which was standing at the up platform at the time, was struck by the blast and many windows were broken throughout the train. Window netting was provided only on the quarter-lights of Unit No. 1413 and these were undamaged.

"It has been ascertained from the local ARP Control that the total casualties were about 40, which figure includes a number of persons alighting from LPTB buses. It has not been possible up to the present to obtain definite information as to who was actually injured on the station or outside the Company's premises, or in the train, but so far as is known, 15 persons at the station received injury and nine of these were conveyed by ambulance to the War Memorial Hospital, Shooters Hill.

"The ambulances, which had been summonsed by the Station master at 8.42 am, arrived at 8.45 am, and all casualties were cleared by 8.55 am. The other six passengers, who were given first-aid treatment by the station staff, i.e. leading Porter Hammond and Female Porter Mrs. Baker, were able to continue their journey after attention.

"The 8.18 am train ex Barnehurst subsequently departed from Eltham (Well Hall) at 8.55 am, and after arrival at Cannon Street the stock was taken out of service and sent empty to Slades Green Depot."

(Sent to R M T Richards to the General Manager).

Even in times of adversity it seems there were still moments when war was momentarily forgotten and instead the opportunity taken for a group photograph. Save for the name of location and date stated, we have no idea as to the occasion, although we know the date - why the number of staff when services at Crystal Palace High Level were at the time suspended? Of particular notice are of course the stored 5BEL Pullman vehicles in the background.

Ray Blanchard / Southwark Model Railway Club (The image was donated to the club approximately 20 years ago.)

A scene for the 1940s, armed forced personnel intermingled with civilian passengers and with the tell-tale alternate stripes on the canopy supports intended as an aid during blackout. The location happens to be Ascot, but it could just as well be anywhere on the SR - or GWR / LMS / LNER.

ST DENYS: 14 AUGUST 1940

"On 14 August 1940, the SR main line between Swaythling and St Denys was cratered by HE and at 17.00 the locomotive working the 15.05 express passenger Bournemouth West - Waterloo fell into it. Trains were diverted *via* Romsey. Three UXB were also found, so delaying repairs. Single line working began after 17 hours with normal working restored after 19½ hours."

The statement made by Driver Lush (62, of Nine Elms) is worth quoting, as an example:- "On Wednesday, 14 August, I booked on duty at 8.50 a.m. I worked the 9.30 a.m. from Waterloo to Bournemouth West and returned with the 3.5 p.m. from Bournemouth West to Waterloo in charge of Engine No. 860 'Lord Hawke' which is a 4-6-0 tender engine of the Lord Nelson Class. The load of the train was 13 vehicles.

"We proceeded from Southampton Central and were stopped at Tunnel Junction and given the 'red' warning of air raid action. I proceeded at 15 miles an hour to St. Denys, where we were booked to stop. After the Station work had been completed we proceeded and after we got to the bridge I heard the noise of a falling bomb. On that I immediately shut the regulator and applied the brake and at the same time heard the noise of the explosion. The whole thing happened almost simultaneously. I did not actually see the road open in front of me [but the fireman did], but I had made an emergency application of the brake. The blast of the explosion seemed to lift us off the footplate and the engine started to rock and settle down. At the same moment the track must have been coming down as the front of my engine pushed a number of the sleepers up together. The engine came to rest in the hole, with the engine and tender in the form of a 'V'. The footplate of the engine was directly over the centre of the hole. I was not hurt. Immediately we stopped, Driver Richards of Eastleigh, who was riding as a passenger in the train, came to the footplate to see if we were all right and if he could assist us. I gave him detonators and flags and asked him to protect the train, whilst I and my mate ballasted the fire to save the boiler. Whilst we were engaged in this heavy gunfire was going on all round us and on one occasion we had to dash to the shelter of the hedge and lie down for some minutes. When the guard came up I think he said he had been knocked down. As far as I know he protected the train. I did not see any signs of panic among the passengers.

"The water out of the tender filled up the hole. I do not think it touched the firebox. I cannot say if it touched the ashbox.

"I was relieved from my engine at 8.0 p.m. and conveyed by light engine to Eastleigh, from which point I got a train home and booked off duty at 11.50 p.m."

The Fireman, William Hone (38, of Nine Elms), confirmed the evidence: "On Wednesday 14 August I came on duty a 8.50 am with driver Lush and worked the 9.30 a.m. Waterloo to Bournemouth west and 3.05 p.m. from Bournemouth west to waterloo. My engine was a Lord Nelson, No. 860.

"We left Southampton Central with a load of 13 bogies and at Tunnel Junction were stopped to be given the 'red' air raid warning action signal. From that point we proceeded at 15 miles an hour and the train is booked to stop at St Denys where we stopped in the usual way. When the station work was completed we carried on under 15 miles an hour and just past the bridge we heard the noise of a falling bomb. My driver said "hold-tight" and he immediately shut the regulator and applied the brake. I was looking through the spectacle glass and saw the track in front of us go up in the air and then the engine fell into the hole and at the same time the sleepers and rails fell down on my side of the boiler.

Lord Nelson, No. 860 'Lord Hawke' in the bomb crater at St Denys. The engine was subsequently re-railed by means of joint effort of the breakdown cranes from Eastleigh and Fratton. The Eastleigh crane travelled to site in the midst of an air raid, the gang pulling down the window blinds as their only means of protection against flying glass. Upon arrival damage to the down line meant the crane could not get close enough to the scene and they had to retire to Swaythling goods yard until the track was repaired. The angle and weight of the locomotive also meant one crane proved insufficient, hence the assistance obtained from Fratton.
Collection of the late W G Bishop.

THE SCENE BEHIND THE SCENE

"I was not hurt with the exception of a very small burn on my left hand.

" When the engine fell into the hole, the engine and tender formed a 'V'. My mate and I had to climb out through the cab. Driver Lush had given me the detonators and flags to protect the down line when driver Richards of Eastleigh, who was travelling in the train, not on duty, came to us and offered his assistance. My driver accepted his offer and Driver Richards went forward and protected the down road, whilst my driver and I ballasted the fire in order to save the boiler. While we were doing this heavy gun fire was going on all around us and on one occasion we had to dash to the shelter of the hedge and lie down for some minutes.

"I saw no sign of panic or excitement among the passengers.

"Driver Lush and I remained by the engine until 8 o'clock when we were relieved and sent to Eastleigh on a light engine to get home."

From the statement of Guard Algar (Southampton Terminus):- "When the bomb went off I was standing up in my van booking the time off St. Denys. At the same moment the driver applied the brake and I went onto the floor. After I had recovered myself a Guard who was travelling spare came back to my assistance. He was Goods Guard Longman of Eastleigh. I gave him detonators and asked him to go up the train and find out how the fireman was, whilst I went back to protect my train. Before I went I asked Ticket Collector Giles to look after the passengers. I went right down to St. Denys Junction signalbox, put down the detonators and returned to the train, after informing the signalman of the circumstances. When I got back to the train the passengers were getting out of the train, but as there heavy gunfire [and] I wanted to get the passengers back into the train and the blinds pulled down. We succeeded in getting the passengers back. At 6.0 p.m. the train was drawn back to Southampton Central, where I was relieved as I was feeling the effects of my fall. I reported for duty the next day."

Finally from the statement by Train Ticket Collector Giles (Bournemouth):- "Almost immediately after leaving St. Denys a bomb dropped on the line and the rain came to a stand. At the time I was riding in the seventh vehicle from the engine. I heard the bomb before it dropped and lay down on the floor of the carriage. After the explosion occurred I got up and went along the corridor to the rear of the train to get my helmet and gas mask. On the way back I found that some of the passengers were still lying on the floor but others had opened the doors and a number of women and children were being assisted out of the train by some soldiers who were travelling on the train. Those persons proceeded to some shelters which were at the end of gardens abutting the railway on the Up side. I should estimate that there were not more than 100 passengers in the train and as I went back to the rear I advised those who had not already alighted to remain in the train and lie down after drawing the window blinds.

When I got to the rear I found that the Guard had just got out of the train to go back and protect it. I said I would go to the front of the train to see about the Driver and Fireman and if the Down Road needed protection. I then proceeded through the train to the front and on the way I met another Guard who was travelling home. I told him that the train guard had gone back to protect the train at the rear and asked him about the front. He said that it had already been done. I went on towards the front to see if anyone required assistance, but no one had any complaint to make. As I was going towards the front I saw Shunter Head, of Southampton Docks, who was travelling on the train. He had the First Aid Box from the front van with him and asked if anyone needed attention. I told him that there was a member of the staff who was in the van at the rear who had a small cut on the left cheek. I understood that Head had already given attention to some passengers who had received minor injuries in the front of the train.

"No one had received any serious injury. There was nothing in the nature of panic amongst the passengers and the majority remained in the train. Those who left did so to proceed to the shelters previously mentioned. I consider that the behaviour of the passengers on the whole was very good."

Sister (or should it be 'brother'?) engine, No. 857 'Lord Howe' in wartime garb, about to depart Platform 3 at Eastleigh towards Swaythling and St. Denys. Two drivers are present, one learning the road.

W Denty collection.

THE EVACUATION THAT NEVER WAS

Contributed by Andrew Harris.

Everyone who has read about the early days of the Second World War will recall the tremendous effort by all the main railway companies in carrying out the evacuation of children from London and other cities to safe areas around the country. The Southern Railway in particular ran 225 trains over three days carrying over 138,000 passengers from London plus over 200 trains from other areas considered vulnerable.

What may not be so well known is the plan for a second mass evacuation, of 'Registered Women and Children', this time dated 'Available for operation any-time from 12.01 am 31 August 1942'. The date is significant, as this was just after the abortive raid of 19 August on Dieppe. The papers covering this second evacuation refer to the 'West Sussex' scheme - geographically Brighton to Littlehampton, but it is likely similar papers were prepared for evacuation of other potential Sussex (and Kent) retaliatory targets. The papers for 'West Sussex Scheme A' refer to 27 pages of pink paper, with a timescale likely to take just a single day. There was also a 'Scheme B', 22 pages on blue paper, for the evacuation of the 'Balance of Population' to be completed in just four days. Both documents make reference to a further 'white copy', (possibly a summary document?) but a copy of this has not been traced.

Dealing with 'Scheme A' it is easy to see how

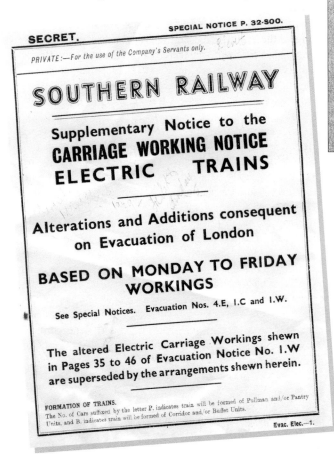

Bottom left - The evacuation we are familiar with, that of 1939.
Top - The forgotten evacuation that was, fortunately, never required.

brilliantly it was arranged. The general instruction being that station masters should make contact with town clerks and that evacuees should arrive marshalled in 'train loads' at appropriate intervals with a 'Station Marshal' provided for entraining and dealing with station staff. A 'Train Marshall' would travel on the train.

Hand luggage only would be allowed with another scheme in hand to allow for a limited quantity of clothing to follow later.

A maximum of 800 passengers were planned for each train, giving a total of 54,650: eight trains scheduled to carry less than 800 figure. A total 72 workings would feature in just one day, each allotted a unique 'Train Number': 201-293 loaded, and 301-377 empty (certain numbers omitted). All trains to be formed of either SR electric main-line or suburban stock. Arrival and departure times and the numbers involved were to be advised to Redhill Control (two to be advised to Woking Control) from each embarkation and detraining station, together with passing times from each of four key intermediate signal boxes. These key locations were, Arundel Junction, Horsham, Three Bridges, and Windmill Junction. Those to Woking were at Havant and Guildford Yard box. Station masters were to provide lists of ordinary trains that wound need to be cancelled although a reduced public service would still run but be liable to be suspended if necessary. (Seven pages were devoted to cancellations on weekdays or dependent upon the starting date Saturday / Sundays, plus details of a limited number of changes where journeys would be altered. A list of the extra staff required at certain stations then followed.)

In addition a number of 'stand-by' trains were to be provided. At Brighton 2 x 12 car. At Hove, 1 x 8LAV. At Ford, 1 x 10COR, all to be manned from 8.00 am to 8.00 pm, whilst at Littlehampton a 12COR was to manned from 8.00 am until noon. Whilst the initial instructions indicate the use of main line / suburban stock, the details above do raise a few questions as to exactly what the make up might be - 10COR especially. There is

PRIVATE and not for circulation.

SOUTHERN RAILWAY — EVACUATION NOTICE No. W.S.B, 1942.

EVACUATION

OF

BRIGHTON, HOVE, PORTSLADE, SOUTHWICK, SHOREHAM, LANCING, WORTHING, GORING, ANGMERING AND LITTLEHAMPTON.

WEST SUSSEX SCHEME "B" —Balance of Population

(For alternative Schemes "W" and "A" see overleaf and separate Notices.)

This Notice is available for operation, when required, as from 12.1 a.m. on 31st August, 1942.

To ensure the smooth and successful working of this important scheme, Station Masters must closely examine and clearly understand the arrangements and satisfy themselves that their Supervisory Staff, Signalmen, and others concerned, are also familiar with them. THIS MUST BE DONE NOW, particularly as when the scheme operates air raids may make conditions difficult and put telephones out of order.

W. J. ENGLAND,
Superintendent of Operation.

O.14764. (2,850).

15

SPECIAL LOADED ELECTRIC TRAINS—*continued.*

Train No.		265	266	269	270	272	273	275	276	278	279	280	281	282
Provision S.X.	Time	8†15	7†50	8†58	8†35	9†20	9†30	10†45	10†40	9†15	12† 2	12†35	12†25	12†49
	From	B'rth.	P. Pk	Brnhm	Bog. R	L.W.	Bog. R	B'ton	Brnhm	Dkg.N.	Lhptn	Lhptn	H Hth	Lhptn
Provision S.O.	Time	8†15	7†50	8†58	8†35	9†20	9†30	10†45	10†40	9†15	12† 2	12†35	12†25	12†49
	From	B'rth	P. Pk	Brnhm	Bog. R	L.W.	Bog. R	B'ton	Brnhm	Dkg.N	Lhptn	Lhptn	H Hth	Lhptn
Provision Sun.	Time	8†15	7†5	8†58	8†35	9†20	9†30	10†45	10†40	9†15	12† 2	12†35	12†25	12†49
	From	B'rth.	P.Pk.	Brnhm	Bog. R	L.W.	Bog. R	B'ton	Brnhm	Dkg.N.	Lhptn	Lhptn	H Hth	Lhptn
To convey		800	800	600‡	800	800	800	800	800	400	800	450	800	800
Head Code	Main Line Stock	86	.07	82	0	03	0	07	0	86	0	41	92	0
	Suburban Stock	P	T	V	O	S	O	T	O	P	O	Ȧ	L	O
		a.m.	a.m.	a.m.	a.m.	a.m.	a.m.	a.m.	a.m.	p.m.	p.m.	p.m.	p.m.	p.m.
Shoreham	dep.	...	...	...	...	10E10	...	...	...	...	...	...	...	...
Lancing	dep.	...	8E20	...	...	...	...	11E20	...	...	...	...	1E20	...
Worthing Ctl.	arr.	...	8/24	...	...	10/20	...	11/24	...	...	...	...	1/24	...
	dep.	...	...	...	9E45	...	10†38	...	11E45	12EP15	12†38	...	...	1E45
W. Worthing	arr.	...	...	...	...	...	10†40	...	...	...	12†40	...	...	...
	dep.	...	...	...	...	...	10E51	...	...	...	12E51	...	...	...
Goring	dep.	...	...	...	...	...	...	...	...	...	...	1E10	...	...
Angmering	dep.	...	...	9E37	...	...	...	...	...	...	...	...	...	...
Arundel Jc.	pass	...	8/36	9/42	9/57	10/34	11/ 1	11/36	11/57	12/27	1/ 1	1/20	1/36	1/57
Littlehampton	arr.	...	...	...	...	...	...	...	...	12 31	...	...	...	...
	dep.	8E35	...	...	...	...	...	...	...	12EP40	...	...	...	...
Ford	arr.	...	...	...	9 59	...	11 3	...	11 59	...	1 3	1 22	...	1 59
	dep.	...	...	...	10 7	...	11 8	...	12 7	...	1 7	1 30	...	2 7
Chichester		...	8/49	9/53	...	10/49	...	11/49	...	...	...	...	1/49	...
Havant	arr.	...	9 5	10 5	...	11 5	...	12 5	...	...	...	...	2 5	...
	dep.	...	9 10	10 10	...	11 10	...	12 10	...	...	...	...	2 10	...
See page		—	17	17	—	17	—	17	—	—	—	—	17	—
Arundel Jc.	pass	8/39	To Esher.	To Guildford and Camberley.	10/ 9	To Chertsey.	11/10	To Malden.	12/ 9	12/44	1/ 9	1/32	To Farnham.	2/ 9
Arundel	pass	8/41			10/12		11/13		12/12	12/47	1/12	1/35		2/12
Itchingfield Jc.	pass	9/ 0			10/33		11/38		12/32	1/11	1/33	1/58		2/38
Horsham	dep.	A9C 4			10C40		11C43		12C39	1C17	1C40	2/ 3		2C43
Dorking N.	arr.	G9/21			11/ 2		12/ 2		12/57	1/35	2/ 2	2DP21		...
	dep.	...			...		...		...	...	...	2 30		3/ 2
Leatherhead		9/27			11/ 8		12/ 8		1/ 3	1/42	2/ 8	2DP37		3/ 8
Epsom	pass	9/32			11/13		12/13		1/ 9	1/48	2/13	...		3/13
Wallington	arr.	...			...		...		...	...	...	...		...
Line		L	—	—	T	—	T	—	T	L	L	—	—	L
Raynes Park	pass	9/45	...	...	11/30	...	12/31	...	1/23	2/ 0	2/33	...	...	3/30
Wimbledon	pass	9/47½	...	...	11/32½	...	...	...	...	2/ 2½	2/37T	...	...	...
E. Putney	arr.	9D55	...	...	...	...	...	...	...	2D10	...	...	...	...
	dep.	10† 5	...	...	...	...	...	...	...	2†20	...	...	...	...
Point Pleasant Jc.	pass	10/ 7L	...	...	...	...	...	...	...	2/22L	...	...	...	...
Clapham Jc.	pass	10/10	...	...	11/37	...	12/37	...	1/30	2/25	2/42	...	...	3/40
Waterloo	arr.	10†17	...	...	11D44	...	12D44	...	1D37	2†32	2D49	...	...	3D48
Disposal S.X.	Time	10†35	—	—	12†15	—	1†14	—	2†15	2†47	3†15	2†55	—	4† 5
	To ...	Port-slade.	—	—	Lhptn	—	South-wick.	—	Wthg Ctl.	Drkg Nth.	Lhptn	Lhptn	—	Port-slade.
Disposal S.O.	Time	10†35	—	—	12†15	—	1†14	—	2†15	2†47	3†15	2†55	—	4† 5
	To ...	Port-slade.	—	—	Lhptn	—	S'wick	—	Wthg Ctl.	W.P.S.	Lhptn	Lhptn	—	Port-slade.
Disposal Sun.	Time	10†35	—	—	12†15	—	1†14	—	2†15	2†47	3†15	2†55	—	4† 5
	To ...	Port-slade.	—	—	Lhptn	—	S'wick	—	Wthg Ctl.	Dorkg. Nth.	Lhptn	Lhptn	—	Port-slade.

A—Precede 8.[illegible] a.m. Bognor Regis from Horsham. G—9.18 a.m. Dorking N. to Waterloo to follow.
DP—Detrain 100 at Dorking North and 350 at Leatherhead. ‡—Detrain 200 at Guildford and 400 at Camberley.
EP—Entrain 100 at Worthing Ctl. and 300 at Littlehampton.

also reference to a 5BEL set to run from Brighton to Victoria, surprising as these units had been withdrawn from service and were then stored at Crystal Palace High Level - *see page 93*.

To avoid conflict and difficulty over track occupancy, trains, generally, originating from locations from Shoreham to Littlehampton set off westwards before turning north. Starting points from Portslade to Hove travelled east before heading north, trains from Brighton itself would go north up the main line. (Certain of the workings envisaged a reversal at Havant.)

Destinations were varied, some never before having had a direct through service from the embarkation point. Amongst the destination stations to be served were Chertsey, Barnes, Esher, Malden, Farnham, Waterloo, East Putney, Leatherhead, Dorking North, Guildford, Camberley, Cannon Street, London Bridge, Victoria and Bagshot.

In the event it was fortunate that none of these evacuations were deemed necessary, although Darwin does refer briefly to 'secret plans' having been put in place for a mass evacuation of 760,000 passengers over four days covering certain areas of the 'East and South Coast'. This does imply there was a similar plan for East Sussex and Kent, perhaps even further along the coast of West Sussex as it is noticeable that Chichester and Bognor were excluded.

This page - *Scheme 'B' and a sample page from evacuation notice. All Andrew Harris collection.*

THE LIGHTER SIDE

Contributed by John Davenport

I have no idea what started me writing down engine numbers at that time. We had lived in a house on the high ground to the west of Woking since December 1933, between the Portsmouth and Southampton lines. The former was nearer but at the bottom of a steep hill, and as traffic was almost totally electric by 1942, the Southampton line was preferred. Helpfully the bike ride to St Johns Hill Road overbridge was almost level, due to the depth of the Goldsworth Hill cutting. On the spotting site was the Tin Bridge, which served both lines just to the west of Woking Junction

My father was a peace-time commuter from Woking. Some time in late 1939 he was told that he would be appointed, along with some of his City colleagues, as a Temporary Civil Servant in the Ministry of Supply, and that would be his wartime occupation. So he continued to commute (the trials of Blitz journeys are another story), and so became known to Mr Avery, the Woking Station Master.

What follows are two pieces of family lore, although they do pre-date my own train spotting. The first was included in 'Return from Dunkirk', by Peter Tatlow, published by the Oakwood Press. Somehow it was discovered that Father could speak French, so when French troops evacuated from Dunkirk were being repatriated via West Country ports, he was asked by Mr Avery to bring any of his friends who could speak French to the station. Along with the W.V.S. and other organisations, he found himself handing out cups of tea and words of encouragement. The trains had come via Redhill and Guildford, and were reversing direction at Woking to head west.

The second story dates to around March 1941. Father was the Chief A.R.P Warden of the western part of Hook Heath. One night when there were German planes about, he was on patrol. At the crossroads on the edge of the escarpment approaching Guildford he met some of the local Home Guard. While they stood there, someone noticed a flashing green light away to the south. There did not seem to be a regular pattern of flashes, but it was highly suspicious. Fortunately one of the party had a compass and various bearings were taken.

As this seemed to be a military matter, it was left to the Home Guard to take further. It was reported next day that the posse had not discovered a nest of spies, rather that it had found Worplesdon Down automatic colour light signals. Even with the projecting hood on the signal head, the light had been visible at some distance, and the intermittent flashing had been caused by branches in the line of sight moving in the wind. That was the family spy story.

Returning now to the more important theme of train spotting, there was then a great shortage of available information. Ian Allan's first Southern ABC appeared in December 1942, so prior to this recording names and numbers was totally haphazard. Fortunately a chance encounter on the railway bridge rescued me. My Deputy Headmaster, Gerald Cannon, was a serious enthusiast and gave me one of his old Southern stockbooks. I also discov-

ered there were two other older railway fans in the school.

The relationship with Mr Avery the station master, got us an invitation to the signal box. Resulting from the 1937 rebuilding of the station and the installation of colour light signalling, it was fascinating. No great crashing levers - it was more like a model railway in operation. The track diagram showed the progress of trains in red lights, while each miniature signal lever had coloured lights above it to show the aspect displayed. There were two signalmen on duty, one at each end of the frame. We were allowed to operate some levers, under strict supervision. There was also enough traffic to be interesting.

Some time in 1943, the three of us from school were asked by Mr Avery whether we would like to visit Feltham marshalling yard. Not surprisingly the answer was yes, so we set off via Weybridge and Virginia Water. On arrival we were given an explanatory talk on how the yard worked and then taken to the signal box controlling one of the humps. The operating system was a mixture of basic procedure and contemporary technology. The signalman had a horizontal track diagram with two push buttons for the control of each set of points. The string of wagons pushed up the hump by the G16 4-8-0T was split into units for each siding by shunters. The number of each required siding was chalked on the end of the first wagon, often on a buffer head. The signalman had to read the numbers and set the appropriate points with little time to spare between each set. It was much too quick for us amateurs and I think we caused the odd miss-sort.

It was now time to eat our sandwiches. And we were shown into a meeting room to do this. Afterwards we hoisted on to the footplate of one of the G16s and given a tour of the yard. We finished up pushing a long train over one of the humps. For a first footplate ride this was most impressive. The power of the locomotive was very apparent with the effort on the fire on each piston stroke as we made steady progress. The general noise was terrific.

Everyone we met was friendly and helpful, and obviously our day had been carefully planned. On the way home we discussed this when one of the party said that while we where having lunch, he had heard two railwaymen talking. From what they said, it was believed we had come from the Southern railway Orphanage at Woking - hence the red-carpet treatment.

As mentioned, our usual base for spotting was at Tin Bridges. Situated immediately to the west of Woking Junction, this crossed all the lines, starting with the down goods shunting and reception tracks and the Portsmouth down and up lines. Such was the divergence between the Portsmouth and Southampton lines, there was about a hundred yards of cinder road to the bridge over the four Southampton tracks. This was a massive piece of LSW engineering with high plate sides. Next to this, at a slight angle, was a newer span with concrete floor and criss-cross girder sides. This was over the two up goods reception roads.

Many engine types remain in the memory, and I suppose we must have seen some of the test runs of the first ten

Ordinary railwaymen at work in extraordinary times. Left is Canterbury West in April 1940, the engine is an R1 No. 1147: the crew of which are standing between the two shunters. On the right is the signalman outside Smeeth 'box in May 1940.

R F Roberts

'Merchant Navy' class and their enormous loads. We also had some of the Riddles WD 2-8-0s appearing regularly after Feltham received an allocation. After D-day these seemed to be one-off appearances in the Down direction. At the time, we assumed, without proof, that these Down direction runs were for getting the engines to a point for embarkation to France having made sure first they were capable of working trains. (The 'R.O' later confirmed this assertion.)

At an earlier date and more unusual, was the down working I saw one Saturday afternoon from St Johns Road Bridge over the Southampton line. There was a lot of noise and eventually around the curve appeared a T14, labouring mightily. Behind it were two dead USA 2-8-0s. I am no technician, but obviously there was some unresolved problem as the 2-8-0s appeared to being hauled against compression. It was quite a spectacle but I doubt that the fireman on the 'Paddlebox' appreciated it.

It was not surprising that there were many unscheduled or unrecognised workings. One which caught my eye was a short train of three Pullman cars and a coach hauled by a T9. It seemed to appear after 4.00 pm on the Up through line and was definitely not stopping at Woking. I thought I would ask some questions to try and find out what we were seeing so often. The reply was along the lines that there were lots of things that were not generally known and it might be wise not to talk too much about what we saw. The train was promptly called the 'Hush Hush' special. (It was in fact the train for the British Airways flying boat service to and from Poole Harbour, running to Victoria via Wimbledon. I cannot recall seeing the Down service, nor recall anything other than a T9 on the working.)

In August 1943 I went to stay with a school friend whose family farmed near Medstead on the Alton - Winchester line. One day we went to Winchester by the M7 push-pull. On the return journey we came into Alresford to find the Down platform occupied by a train of LMS coaches. To our surprise and interest, it was full of American soldiers. The window was down at once and we had a few moments conversation over the gap. This train moved off almost immediately, but as it went a shower of goodies shot through the window. Definitely a help for Anglo-American relations.

In addition to Mr Avery the Woking Station master mentioned earlier, there was a family friend whose railway contacts were invaluable. Known to us as 'The Colonel' he was a Lieutenant Colonel, R.E. (Retired) with a lifelong interest in railways and access to every level of the Southern's management. He arranged a visit to Clapham Junction 'A' signal box (the one controlling the Waterloo lines) for the two colleagues of the Feltham adventure and myself. The magnitude of traffic and the work of the signalmen was impressive. Woking box seemed very pedestrian in comparison. A slight distraction from the explanations we were given was the appearance of steam on the Victoria lines, including Atlantics and I3 4-4-2Ts.

The Colonel's most exclusive excursion was one for which the beginning and end are infuriatingly indistinct. It was in the winter of 1943 that I had a private tour of Nine Elms shed. I remember it was raining and after the bomb damage conditions was filthy. The sheds were full of engines, mostly familiar ones. There were two, however, of which they seemed to be proud. The first was their D1 0-4-2T (I believe No. 2220) fitted out as a mobile fire pump. As these were rather ineffective unless attached to a mains supply, I am not sure why it was an icon. The second was more mysterious. At the back of one of the sheds in a corner was a carefully shrouded object. I was invited to look under the covering around what was the cab area. Underneath in all its glory was No. 119, the Southern's Royal engine, still beautifully polished and gleaming.

I have since worked out that my guide for some of this visit might have been J Pelham-Maitland, the Nine Elms Shedmaster. Unfortunately I cannot remember how I got to or from Nine Elms, but the actual visit was unforgettable.

What might be called the 'Doodlebug Summer' of 1944 produced restrictions on our travel to London, which were probably sensible. In fact our 'personal ' V1 fell at the bottom of the hill close to the Portsmouth Line, fortunately on nursery land.

One consequence of D-Day was the appearance of Ambulance Trains to no set timetable. As far as I can remember they were hauled by their allocated LNER B12s. One train was stabled at the far north of the Up sidings by Tin Bridges where there was also crew accommodation. I do not recall seeing the train's arrival or departure. A mental picture that has stayed with me all these years is of the train in its siding on a sunny evening, the Red Cross emblems on white squares on the roof of each coach showed up clearly, while the smoke from the chimney of the crews quarters rose straight into the air. It seemed so peaceful compared to what was going on across the channel.

A major day out in April 1945 was a visit to Eastleigh shed and the sidings for engines awaiting the works. I have checked both the 'Railway Observer' and the 'Railway Magazine' for the period but it does not seem to have been a public event; it must have probably been down to the Colonel. In all there were 64 western section engines, as well as visitors from Ashford, St Leonards, and Exmouth Junction.

Much of the factual matter associated with these memories has been checked in the various books by the late D L Bradley. I would emphasize that it worked that way round - I did not read Bradley to find out what I should have seen. I am sure there was a great deal that I missed, and probably some misinterpretation. In mitigation I would plead that school was six days a week in term-time, there was a war on, and my fourteenth birthday was not until October 1945. But I can still hear that T14 struggling with the two USA 2-8-0s and see the T9 gliding round the curve with the Pullmans. Just don't ask me to recall what I was doing last week….!

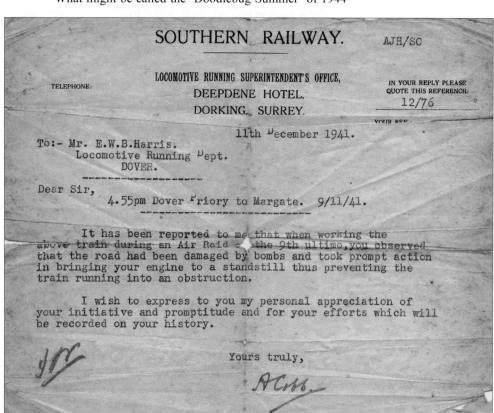

Left - One example - this a surviveor from a precious family archive - describing the actions of one man that could otherwise so easily have been forgotten.
Courtesy Jeremy O'Keeffe

Opposite left - Another example of WW2 paperwork.
Submitted by Gregory Beecroft.

Opposite right - Some things carried on just as normal during wartime. The only exception is the female staff, seen in the bowels of Waterloo with a batch of lost property.

FEEDBACK.....

As with any book new / revised information will come to light - usually just after publication! The following has been received with grateful thanks;.

From Mr C R Berridge - "Part 1 in the series, pages 26 and 27, the locomotive type should be described as an 'N'. In Part 2, the double page spread on pages 2/3 shows the railwaymen wearing a heavy duty type gas-mask. These can be identified by having separate eye pieces. Page 61 shows a member of the U1 class. Page 64 depicts damage to No. 917 'Ardingly'. Driver Cotton from Ramsgate was killed in this incident: he had been one of the enginemen on No. 934 'St Lawrence' when it was inspected by the College's boys in 1935. The actual bomb incident occurred at Deal.

Pages 66-68 show the damage to D3 No. 2365. According to 'Kent at War' the date is given as 27 November. Driver C Gilbert suffered shock and Fireman Albert hills was scalded.

Page 155 - I would suggest that the date could not be 1943. The ship would have been painted grey and might by then have had the large gantry over the stern; there would not have been the interested crowd, I doubt if civilians on that scale would have been allowed into Dover Docks."

From Mr Tony Logan - "What for instance is J2 4-6-2T No. 2326, old 'Bessborough', doing in Nine Elms loco? The pictures emphasise the craftsmanship involved in getting locos and stock back into service good as new. On Page 120 the wrecked bridge is over Southwark Street. I have seen the illustration before somewhere and there are others of the same incident in the 2007 Capital Transport book 'London Main Line War Damage', pp 84, 85 and 101. The train must be one of the first to use the bridge, rebuilding is far from complete. The '3' unit visible is one of the group 1631-57 formed of ex-LBSC steam stock on new SR underframe (looks like 1651 or possibly 1631). It's on its way towards Blackfriars (the old LCDR station on the south bank is visible). Lewes Road viaduct - judging by the cab profile the 4-4-2T is an I 1X. 'Peverill Point' is the only Brighton Atlantic that evaded me, no time was lost in breaking it up, unlike No. 2040 which languished for a long time on the scrap road before being moved to Kimbridge Junction and Dinton for scrapping. The 'London Railway Record' recently had some views of Lordship Lane where a V1 with its engine still running scored a direct hit on the subway. One railwayman is reported as being killed there even though the service had been suspended since 22 May 1944 for the duration."

From Vivian Orchard - Part 2, page 44. "The engine is not departing with 20-coach test train. I suspect it is getting it all together. It is backing into the station, hence the solenoid shunt signal being off. The exhaust blow at the front of the engine would also indicate it was going backwards. It must have been an operational headache."

From David Butler, reference the view of Hayes station after bombing, Page 87 of Part 1, this was a German bomber which was being pursued by two British Spitfires with bits falling off it. Unfortunately it crashed on to what was an almost new station causing two fatalities.

SOUTHERN RAILWAY   SPECIAL NOTICE No. S.O.O. 36, T.

SPECIAL MILITARY TRAFFIC ARRANGEMENTS

SECOND DAY.

REFERENCES.

Reference.	Explanation.	Reference.	Explanation.
†	Empty train.	T	Through Line.
L	Local Line.	‖	Light Engine.
M	Main Line.	W	Calls for Water.

152906—1—**2nd DAY.**

DAMAGE and DISRUPTION on the RAILWAYS of GREAT BRITAIN during WORLD WAR TWO

B.W.L. BROOKSBANK

DAMAGE and DISRUPTION on the RAILWAYS
of GREAT BRITAIN during WORLD WAR TWO
B.W.L. BROOKSBANK

CONTENTS

1.

INTRODUCTION
Table of Analysis of Reports of Damage and Delay by Enemy Action, 1940 – 1945   3.
Table of Analysis of Casualties due to Enemy Action on Railway Property   5.
Preparations   7.
Coping with Disruption
AIR ATTACKS ON BRITAIN
The 'Phoney War', September 1939 – May 1940
The Onset of 'Real War', June – September 6 1940
Table of Railway Incidents, June – December   9.

7 June – 6 September 1940
London (Civil Defence Region No. 5)
Southeast and South (Regions 6 and 12)
Eastern Counties (Region 4) and Lincolnshire – part of Region 3
Southwest (Region 7)
Wales (Region 8)
Midlands (Region 9)
North Midlands (Region 3, excluding Lincolnshire)
Northwest (Region 10)
Yorkshire, East and West Ridings (Region 2)
Northeast (Region 1)
Scotland (Region 11)

LONDON, Autumn 1940   17.
Saturday 7 – Sunday 8 September 1940: the Beginning of London's Ordeal   21.
9 – 30 September 1940   31.
October 1940   41.
November 1940   46.
December 1940   49.

PROVINCES, Autumn 1940   49.
MAIN RAIDS: 51.
Southampton and Portsmouth (September – December)   51.
Plymouth (November – December)   54.
Bristol and Avonmouth (September – December)   59.
Merseyside (August – December)   61.
Manchester (August – December)   68.
Midlands (October – December)   69.
Sheffield (December)
MISCELLANEOUS, September – December
Southeast and South
Eastern Counties and Lincolnshire
Southwest
Wales
Midlands
North Midlands
Northwest
Yorkshire, East and West Ridings
Northeast
Scotland

Another serious incident entailed heavy damage to **Brompton & Fulham Goods** (WLER), where two staff were killed. A UXLM at **Old Oak Lane Halt** stopped Birmingham line traffic for 10 hours from 23.15 (16/4). Fenchurch Street to Shoeburyness: after 1½ hours the rest of the train was taken on to Hornchurch by an engine off an Up **LMSR**.- At **Upney** at 23.10, HE made a crater into which fell the locomotive and first coach of the 22.30 OP freight; the steam lines were clear by 17.40 next day, the LPTB electric lines: 24 hours later. Meanwhile however, at 03.40 (17/4) HE exploded on a District Line train at **Elm Park**, blocking all four lines for 36 hours (steam) to 87 hours (electric) – but no casualties were reported. On the other LT&S line at **Dagenham Dock**, extensive damage to buildings and stock was caused by HE and by the delayed explosion of a land-mine at 02.00. Nevertheless, steam trains continued Shoeburyness – Tilbury – Barking, with a shuttle Barking – Hornchurch; NWR at 18.00 20/4.

On the NLR, firstly **Brondesbury Park** Station was put out of service at 00.45. Next, at **Broad Street** at 03.00, HE penetrated the platform to the stables and killed several horses. Then at 04.30, blast and fire damaged arches and the track at **Haggerston**, blocking the lines and injuring one staff. All trains were then terminated at Dalston Junction and although one line was cleared for freight after seven hours, no passenger trains were run to Broad Street for a week. Extensive damage was done also at **Old Ford Yard** and to the Stations at **West End Lane and Chalk Farm**. Incidents on other LMS lines that night were minor, although one staff was injured fire-fighting at **St Pancras**.

LNER.- One staff was injured at 22.30 by IB at **Finsbury Park**. Great damage was done at 00.15 to **Stratford Works**, after a direct hit on the Boiler Shop. Also three signalboxes and **Carpenters Road Depot** were damaged, along with 170 carriages in **Channelsea Sidings**, the Channelsea Curve being blocked for eight hours. There was extensive damage done at major Goods Depots: at **Marylebone Goods**, where the warehouse was gutted and 80 cartage vehicles destroyed, two staff were injured and the Depot was closed, after using emergency facilities at Neasden and Wembley Exhibition, a new loading platform was built for Marylebone on Barge Road to handle shed traffic. At **Farringdon Goods**, the High Level was largely destroyed, and owing to damage and fires in buildings adjacent, the MWL were closed at 03.45 for 12 hours. Excluding the great quantities of stored goods destroyed, the damage to these Depots was assessed at £714,000 (£18m today) and £155,000 (£4m today), respectively. Much damage was done also at **Bishopsgate Goods**. At **King's Cross**, the C&W Shops were destroyed.

On the **SR**, all the passenger termini had to be closed.
SR, Western Section.- At **Waterloo**, bombs were falling all around at 22.30, and at 23.00 the Station was closed and owing to HE on the tracks near **Vauxhall** all traffic to Clapham Junction was stopped. The **Necropolis Station** was destroyed, with four coaches burnt out (including the funeral train) and one staff injured. At 00.05, the front of **Vauxhall** Station (refreshment room and Parcels office) was blown out, with debris thrown over the Windsor Lines. By 01.00, six lines **Waterloo – Clapham Junction** were blocked by HE at no less than six places, including at Wandsworth Road Bridge. Only the two Main Local lines were left usable and at **Queen's Road** all eight lines were blocked, but the Main Line side was clear by 03.55, the Windsor Lines an hour later. At 03.00, further HE had damaged all four Windsor Lines again near **Vauxhall** and the traction current was off as far as Clapham Junction. By 04.55 there were no lights or power, so HSW was in operation – for such steam movements as were needed. Further HE in the night blocked the Windsor Lines – mainly.

Local trains were turned round at Earlsfield, but access to the terminus was available for steam trains from 12.00 17/4 – via East Putney and the Up Windsor Local Line. By 15.00 18/4, the Down and Up Main Local lines were open – in daylight only, and the first train out of Waterloo left at 16.07. Happily, no further damage was done in the raid of 19-20/4, but the signalling remained out of order until 22-23/4 and TBW had to be employed. By 12.50 on 20/4, the Main Through lines were clear to Clapham Junction; eight trains per hour were being run, but on the Local lines only old 'B' Box, it was not so on to were run per hour, but although signalling and tracks were in order as far as the site of the old 'B' Box, it was not so on to Loco Junction. By 10.30 on 22/4, the four Windsor Lines were largely in order, but repairs to adjacent lines and to arches, also problems with signalling, meant that they were not fully reopened for another 10 – 14 days – albeit just in time for the last great raid on 10/5 (see below).

Beyond Clapham Junction there were further problems. On 18/4 at 16.05, a DAB was found at **Earlsfield** and the lines were out of alignment. Through services were suspended, and a shuttle service run Waterloo – Clapham Junction, buses being provided Clapham Junction – Wimbledon. Then at 17.10, another UXB was reported 50 yards from the Down side at **Earlsfield**. Steam trains were then run via East Putney to Clapham Junction (Windsor side), shunting there via the Yard onto the Up Main Local to continue to Waterloo! On 19/4, a screen of wagons was placed on the Down Through line and the Local lines reopened at 15.15. The Main Through lines at **Nine Elms Loco Shed** two locomotives overturned and badly damaged[19]; the bodies of a driver and a fireman were discovered and removed that afternoon. About 15 HE fell at **Nine Elms Goods Yard**, mainly in the Up side yard, damaging numerous buildings, sidings and wagons, also several road vehicles, cranes and other equipment; all sidings were back in use by 28/4. At **East Putney**, the Station buildings were damaged and the lines blocked towards Southfields, but in spite of a UXB on top of **West Hill Tunnel**, LPTB services resumed at 13.00 on 18/4 (under SpR for a week).

SR, Central Section.- At 00.20, damage was done by HE at **London Bridge** and all lines to **New Cross Gate** were blocked after a large crater was found in the Local lines; all were clear in 14½ hours. At the same time, all lines were

179   'Lord Nelson' 4-6-0 No. 852 'Sir Walter Raleigh' and 'Schools' 4-4-0 No. 927 'Clifton'.

The CD –ROM opposite contains a numbered, 230 page, searchable PDF file of incidents and occurrences of damage and disruption on the SR, GWR, LMS, LNER and LPTB systems during World War Two.

Separate Contents and Index files are provided, again in PDF form. In addition there are over 160 images, arranged broadly in chronological order of relevance to the events recorded in the text.

This work is the result of considerable research into the official records held at the National Archives, Kew: relevant source notes are provided within the text. A large selection of images from contemporary photographs, held in the files at the National Archive is appended as separate folders upon the CD.

Part of Ben Brooksbank's work has been published previously in BACKTRACK between 2000 and 2006 and in his books 'TRIUMPH AND BEYOND, THE EAST COAST MAIN LINE 1939 - 1959, PART ONE': Challenger 1998, and 'LONDON MAIN LINE WAR DAMAGE': Capital Transport 2007. This cumulative archive, however, brings together the published work and also extends it to the whole of Great Britain (but not Northern Ireland). Included for the first time are numerous disruptive events on the Railways not directly related to enemy action.

The archive has been deposited with the Imperial War Museum for open presentation as a PDF in their 'Collections on Line', but without the illustrations. It has also, together with 75 of the images, been presented as a PDF to members (and their friends) of the World War Two Railway Study Group.

Should the content be used elsewhere, acknowledgement to Dr. B.W.L. Brooksbank is requested.